DESTINY'S DAUGHTER

LYNDA FILLER

It was the best of times. I was in love.
And the worst of times. I was afraid that
love would be the death of me.

Quotes from Lynda's other memoirs by readers' reviews.

Love The Beat Goes On

"This book charts an incredible journey from dis-ease to ease and, however skeptical you may be about Lynda's methods, the proof is still here, still writing, 13 years after being told to "put her affairs in order." That is indisputable and breathtaking!" Lisa

"Powerful and unforgettable" JackMagnus, 5 Star Readers' Favorite

"This is a book every human alive should read and take away the lessons given. If I could give it ten stars, I would. It's that good." Jan Sikes

Café Confidential

A Stunning tale of a life well-lived.

"I don't know Lynda, but after reading her Cafe Confidential I wish I did. Her story is completely amazing and inspiring, and she tells it with such honesty you feel like you are sitting side by side in a Turkish Starbucks, sipping delicious grande cappuccinos and sharing secrets. From healing drums to covid tragedies, the narrative bears the full weight of heartfelt emotion and authenticity. And all along the way she supports and is supported by her outlook on life and some lifelong friends. I can't recommend this book highly enough. It will stay with you long after you reach the final paragraph. It may even change your life." H. Hackett

"Sad when the book was over."

"I loved the 1st book. And was so excited to find out she had written a second one. I was hoping there was a 3rd but sadly there wasn't. I've read many books that were page turners but none like this one. This is a soul sister someone my age with my experiences and I couldn't get through it fast enough! I can only hope that she writes a 3rd memoir." Mary Lynne

DESTINY'S DAUGHTER

I was born into a Canadian military family. Wanderlust was in my genes.

In 2019 I sold everything I owned and traveled solo to Europe, the Middle East and Asia. I celebrated my 72nd birthday listening to a bomb explode in Tel Aviv. But it wasn't until I found love with a very young Turkish man in Istanbul that I knew I had crossed a point of no return.

Three love-filled years later it was inevitable that the Covid lockdown and the fear of an unknown future had already caused incredible stress. But when I witnessed the Russian Warships return home along the Bosphorus Strait I questioned if my wanderlust would turn out to be the biggest mistake of my life.

Vulnerability

Brené Brown says it best:

"Owning our story can be hard but not nearly as difficult as spending our lives running from it. Embracing our vulnerabilities is risky but not nearly as dangerous as giving up on love and belonging and joy—the experiences that make us the most vulnerable. Only when we are brave enough to explore the darkness will we discover the infinite power of our light."

TABLE OF THOUGHTS

1

IT'S BEEN A BUSY TIME IN
HEAVEN AND HELL.

When man plans, God laughs.

It's over two long years since whispers of a deadly virus became news. It was subtly stated that an unusual, seemingly incurable virus was causing concern in medical circles. It was linked to several deaths, and it was spreading quickly.

When I first read about this insidious disease, I was seated in this exact spot on my metal café chair on the 2 x1meter patio of my fourth-floor flat in Istanbul. I made the immediate decision to self-isolate. I was a survivor of an 'incurable' heart condition in 2008, and I was not taking any chances. As I watched the massive international container ships navigate the busy Bosphorus Strait, I wondered when and if this frightening illness would attack Istanbul, a city of more than sixteen million people.

I had a conversation with myself. Istanbul, one of the largest international cities in the world, is home to both Turks and refugees from several war-torn countries. Even though my health is good, I never know when my heart might decide to go on strike again! Rather than take chances, if I stay inside, this disease will probably blow over in a few weeks. Once the doctors get the virus under control, I can always return to my 'normal' life.

Towards the end of February 2020, I welcomed my boyfriend Yunus Emre as he unpacked his car filled with the basic necessities that he thought I might need, plus my two non-perishables, cases of water and cans of diet coke. I make no apologies for my disgusting cola habit. I'll blame it on Coca-Cola commercials I watched on TV when I was younger.

Who is Yunus Emre, you ask? He's the reason I'm in Istanbul, Türkiye. While my friend, Emre carried everything to the elevator of my small apartment building, I thought about his life. I'd recently learned he began working at the age of fourteen. I assumed he was a bad boy who refused to go to school. He probably hung out with other like-minded souls, smoked pot, and eyed the girls. But that was not the case. His four brothers and their parents had moved from a small village near Gaziantep in Türkiye to the big city of Istanbul. Hopefully it would be a chance for a better life. He's the youngest, but everyone must work. When I met Emre, he worked during the day, studied at night school, and wrote exams to complete high school. I'm humbled and ashamed that I jumped to conclusions from my view of the world and not the reality of another's life.

I had a lot of lessons to learn in this country, and that was only one. But I'm getting ahead of myself. All my travels to Europe, Asia, the Middle East, and now Türkiye brought this Canadian girl to Istanbul and life in a Muslim country. I never planned on living here. But if I'm candid, I had retired from my day job in Mexico to travel and write. Beyond that, I had no plan.

I looked at my guy, and my heart was full. I was grateful for him and the love he brought into my life. Little did we know that three months later, in May of 2020, this terrifying Covid-19 disease would grab hold of him, two of his brothers, and his mother, who would all heal. But within twelve hours of my message from Emre, Covid would kill his beloved father.

2

ARMY BRAT

The statute of limitations on blaming our parents never wears out, right?

My father was a sergeant major in the Canadian Army, and every three years, we would get a new posting. It sounds rather glamorous, but I wonder if the military has ever studied the damage that all this change might have done to families. You learn to make friends but stay aloof because everything, especially friendship, is temporary. You will need to move on and form new relationships three years from now. And it wasn't only 'best friends' that suffered. It became impossible to grow up with familial relationships that last. My cousins, aunts, and uncles all lived back in Eastern Canada.

My mother's family circa 1940, The Curtin's and the Callaghan's

I have three siblings; my youngest passed away a few years ago, my older brother lives in British Columbia, and my sis is in Ottawa. I'm the wanderer. I have no place I call home. I realize how my nomadic upbringing made it possible to walk away from failed relationships and marriages. Starting over was in my genes, like the freckles on my face, my once-red hair, and chubby legs. I was too young to understand the emotional disconnect and eventual damage that found a home in my physical heart until it was almost too late.

I will skip a few decades and bring you into the eighties. After a couple of failed relationships, I found the one to create my own family. When you move to areas like Whistler, BC, and bring up your boys in a ski resort, you live the dream. For several years I lived a normal family life. I'm not a winter person, but I loved selling the lifestyle for other families to travel to exotic international places on vacation. My career flourished. And my boys grew up in a healthy, active community.

Ski-resort–living can get tiresome, along with an unfulfilling marriage. But it takes two to marry and two to break up a marriage. It could have been my restless spirit or the belief that there must be more to life than a constant bickering relationship. But run away, I did. I'd learned from childhood to pack a suitcase and move on. I followed the sun and in the early 2000's I moved to Mexico.

West Coast Puerto Vallarta, Mexico

It's now twenty years later, and time to retire from my day job in sales. I'd also followed another dream of mine and had begun to publish my writing. My boys are adults and live in Vancouver, Canada, and Paris, France. But what does retirement look like? I've worked my entire adult life in fashion and then travel. I've lived in fabulous places. But I've never been fortunate in love. Or maybe I make choices that are doomed from the start. Either way, I no longer have anyone to answer to, so I can do what I want and not hurt anyone. So, what to do?

I'd like to say I thought this out. But I didn't really. I'd had a far too close call with death in 2008—an incurable heart condition that I was blessed with healing. In some ways, I had no excuse for not making whatever years I have left on this planet the best years of my life. This restlessness led me to wake up one morning and liquidate my life in Mexico.

I've discovered that when change is right, everything aligns. My condo was sold to the first person who saw it. I never even put it on the market. I sold my paintings. And my favorite art is in my friend Jeanne's home in Mexico so I can look at it when I visit her. I organized my finances, packed one suitcase, and bought a series of one-way plane tickets. I was off to see exotic cities and islands I'd only read about or seen in movies.

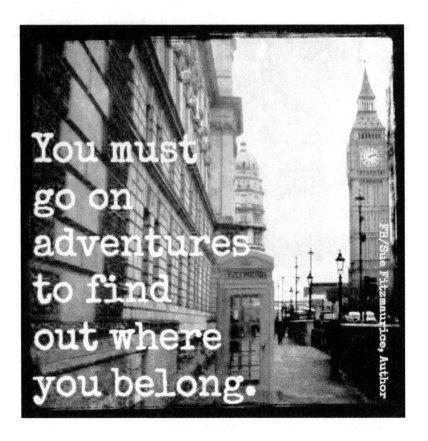

You must go on adventures to find out where you belong.

FB/Sue Fitzmaurice, Author

"It will be easy." I told myself, "You've done this so many times before!"

And I have. However, I would travel by myself to places I'd never visited except in my imagination. I simplified my trip with no return tickets. Everything of value was either in my suitcase, bank account, or forever implanted in my heart. I had no firm plan of what would happen when I used up the last ticket in my knapsack. But as it had in the past and would continue to do in the future, my heart would lead the way. This would turn out to be my *Eat Pray Love* journey, although I didn't know it at the time.

To understand the present, I will share some of the past with you and the insights that led me to write this third memoir. I invite you to join me with a cup of tea, or a glass of wine, while I sip my coffee in a café in Istanbul, Türkiye.

The magic waits
just outside
your
comfort zone
LOVE The Beat Goes On   Lynda Filler

3

A CURSE AND A BLESSING

During my career in sales, I dealt with people all day long. Technology allowed me to continue to interact when I wanted to and turn it all off when I didn't feel like being part of an electronic social world. It also continues to offer me a platform to explore my creativity. I'm able to connect with friends, followers, and creatives worldwide.

In Mexico I would find my international tribe. It was Myspace in the early days. We wrote our poetry, poured our hearts out, and fell in love and lust. It was all safe, faraway relationships that we knew could/would never go anywhere. A perfect place for an incurable romantic to express her angst in a physically secure environment. As far as the emotional heart goes, that would be another matter altogether.

I was inspired to create when I became a woman scorned or had enigmatic relationships with people who portrayed themselves to be anything and anyone that captured their imaginations. I let that poison drip from my typing fingertips in poetry. There were no safeguards. Fake personas populated the Myspace site alert for victims to charm and play the game of love. It was exhilarating and inspiring. It could also be nasty and sometimes painful. But at times, it was fabulous. And that's what I choose to remember.

I took the best of what I wrote during those days and published three books of poetry on Amazon. The Love Fix, Love Rehab, and I (Spy) Love. I can re-read those books today and see that life did leave some scars, although they are barely visible anymore.

The most exhilarating byproduct of all this poetic drama? It gave me the confidence to begin publishing prose. I began with my first memoir in 2015 and several fiction books followed. With this third memoir, I will now have twenty books on Amazon. A word of caution: you know what they say about an author? Don't make her angry. You will end up in one of her novels, or worse, in a memoir. And how you treat her will determine your fate! I wonder how many of my acquaintances see themselves as heroes or villains in my novels.

My **Code Raven Series** is based on people from divergent backgrounds who showed up to play online in the Myspace days— the precursor of Facebook. My vivid imagination took those characters, made them spies and ex-Seals, and enhanced their lives to create a fun, exciting, dramatic series. One of the key members is a bad-ass female named Samaar. The Raven group go around the world fighting evil and righting the world's wrongs. Drama, action, love—what more do we want, right?

The knowledge I acquired about the Universe we inhabit inspired something deeper. Although I'd lived in Canada, Mexico, and for short periods of time in the USA, I knew very little about the world. In the last few years, I've learned that if the world is to survive, we must realize ***We are all one***. Those words would become a theme in my writing and a conviction in my life.

4

PAST FORWARD

When you carry the past forward, we call it *baggage*. But let's think of the following few paragraphs as "carry-on" luggage.

Emotional baggage can get extremely heavy over the decades. Letting go is done through intention and sometimes therapy. Or, in my case, I simply have a selective memory. But buried old wounds can sneak up on you until all your current actions become reactions to past events. And nothing will age you faster than an endless list of regrets.

I share my background to reference where and why I can pack up and move the same way you might prepare an overnight bag for a weekend in the mountains. It's a stoic approach to military life honed over years of not saying goodbye but acting as if this new adventure was my idea. Today it's left me with very few comfortable memories of my past that I can go to when I need them. Instead, it's as if I've lived so many lifetimes I wonder who I am. I'm not complaining. It's more an observation or explanation of why I seem to settle in exotic places. It's my version of 'homeless.'

My creative outlets have saved my life over the years. If it was a romance I must get over, an unfulfilling job, or even a business that must close, I've developed mechanisms to get me through it all. *I've got this*, I would tell myself. And usually, my therapy would be to lose myself in a good book or write it all out. It worked—until it didn't.

I go far when I run away from home. I've lived in Ottawa, Montreal, Toronto, Whistler, BC, Puerto Vallarta, Mexico, and I'm currently in Istanbul, Türkiye. I would call myself the Queen of Starting Over. It's how I learned to cope as a child. The military gives you no option. You've got to go. You say goodbye to your friends. Then pack up a suitcase. The movers take the big things. And you hold your head high, learn not to cry, and look toward a new life and home in a faraway city.

As a child in a military family, I learned a life-saving lesson. If things don't work out and you've tried your best to fix it, move on. I thought moving on would be more effortless and less damaging. But that's not how nature works. And it's certainly not how my heart responded. I simply didn't know it at the time.

By 2007 I had lived in Mexico for several years. I'd fallen in love more than once. I like to be in love. It's thrilling, exciting, exhilarating—until it's not. How often can you break your heart without expecting your heart to go on strike? But I wasn't thinking about my heart at this point. I needed to switch it up. Life has always had a way to read my mind. It's as if my aura is so powerful that the annoying voice inside my head gets tired of listening to me and presents me with options.

I received a call from my ex-employer, Intrawest, in Whistler, BC. I They wanted their *top closer, super manager* (in my humble opinion), to return for the winter season. It wasn't in my plans. But I didn't have anyone I was involved with in Mexico, so I was mobile. I had begun to chat with someone who lived somewhere in the Pacific Northwest so that was a plus. Even though Whistler was the number one ski resort in North America, I didn't care about the skiing. But I do like to live in resort areas. I was ready for a change.

The company made it almost impossible for me to say no. No matter what I asked for, they said yes. All my travel expenses would be paid. Accommodations would be provided *gratis*, and I had a great management position. I would work with people I knew and a boss I loved. So, I packed up my car, rented out my newly purchased condo, and began the ten-day solo drive from Puerto Vallarta, Mexico, to Whistler, British Columbia. I shared this journey in my first memoir, **LOVE the Beat Goes On**.

View from my condo in Puerto Vallarta, Mexico

I know you can't move forward if you always look backwards. But I look back to revisit and remind myself of my lessons. And to share them with you. On this two-week drive up the West Coast, I learned how incredibly fortunate I am.

Before I began this epic drive, I experienced several sinus infections. I had no idea why. I blamed it on the humid, moist, and sometimes moldy summer climate near the ocean in Mexico. Other than one suitcase, I bought extra sinus meds and began my two-week drive up the Pacific coast of Mexico, the USA, and finally into British Columbia, Canada.

Whistler, British Columbia 2008

Whistler, BC, Canada, the late summer of 2008

I loved every moment of that journey. I now realize that a woman that decides to travel thousands of miles on her own might not have thought out the whole journey. But I wasn't thinking of the negatives. I looked forward to the challenge and excitement of my winter contract in Canada. I only had one problem. The sinus medicine I had been on for the past couple of months was not doing its job.

I arrived in Whistler, BC, and before I began to work, I found it difficult to breathe. At first, I blamed it on the altitude. In time I would adjust. And then, a couple of weeks after I began to work, I was settled in my new chalet and went out to explore the town. I had another "sinus" attack where I couldn't breathe. I remember exactly where I was when I sat down on a snow-covered step. Suddenly, it hit me. This is not a sinus infection. It's a heart attack!

I should have stopped someone and asked for an ambulance, *Instead I waited for the shortness of breath to pass.* I've always believed I'm surrounded by angels. Maybe my parents or family watch over me from wherever they are in the afterlife. I assume there is an afterlife. Some days the jury is out on all of that too. But I know with the luck I've had in my life, there must be angels. I waited for my breath to return to normal. Then I walked ten minutes to the nearby local clinic. Yes, I walked. What was I thinking? It must be a Baby Boomer belief that we are immortal!

I know today how incredibly fortunate I was to receive warnings. I didn't get it the first time. The Universe said, "let's *continue to zap her until she realizes she has had a heart attack!"* My local doctor had a general idea of what was wrong and gave me a referral to a Cardiologist in the city for quick tests. In the meantime, he gave me pills to take that would stop the attacks. It turned out that

I would be diagnosed with Idiopathic Dilated Cardiomyopathy, an enlarged heart. But the Idiopathic part meant they had no idea why.

Sometimes I tend to gloss over the bad things in my life. When you hit your seventies, as I have, you have lived a long life. The mind has far too many details to sift through, so we might as well let some of the thoughts be forgotten. That's my theory. After all, we are not machines. Well, maybe our bodies and our minds are machines. But this machine was built in 1947, and although I still see myself as a sleek, sexy, and far-too-flirty operating device, the reality might be slightly different!

In 2008 my heart said, "No more. There are consequences to your love actions."

I grew up during the women's liberation movement. We are the generation that believed we could do and have it all. Yes, we burned out. We divorced, and we became single parents; we took over the financial responsibilities for our family. And some, like me, left our teenage kids with their fathers and went to 'find' ourselves. To this day, I make no excuses for my actions. Could I have made better choices? Maybe. But I know I can't move forward, stay healthy, and have a sound mind if I'm always blaming myself for the learning lessons that others might call mistakes. I love myself with all my faults. I'm simply a woman trying to cope in a world very different than my mother's and more than likely, different than the one you will face in your generation.

We have no role models to help us navigate this modern world. We are an open society, and we share so much on social media. We are bombarded with stories about the life of the rich and famous. But that's not necessarily your life or mine. I hope I can help you understand that you are never alone. There is always someone experiencing similar things. Find your tribe. Some of us have found it on FB in Lynda's Raven Army. Many of my 'tribe' have been with me for forty years! I'm super grateful for the support I receive daily. But you also need a "real" tribe. Friendships that will be there for you while you navigate the minefields. I hope my story will help you figure out aspects of your life that confuse you or hurt you. And more than that, in my writing and your reading, we can find a way to open our hearts to the vulnerability we will need to move forward in this convoluted universe we live in today.

the life you have led doesn't need to be the only life you have.

ANNA QUINDLEN

5

BAGGAGE IS FOR TRAVEL

The winter of 2007 and onward, I drove back and forth from the mountains of Whistler to Vancouver city to see the Cardiac Specialist. I chose not to tell anyone I had a problem. My co-managers understood I had a health issue I would need to look after. I explained there would be days when I would have to go to Vancouver—a two-hour drive—but I'd be happy to make up the time on other days. They understood. My performance at work was solid, and they were glad to have me. Whatever I had to deal with, I would go and return the same day to Whistler.

The Cardiologist added to my medications. But from the moment I took my first pill in Whistler at the GP's office, I never had an attack again. We did test after test. Finally, the Cardiologist explained to me that I had Idiopathic Dilated Cardiomyopathy. In layman's words, an enlarged heart but the Idiopathic means the doctors have no idea why.

"Is it curable?"

The doctor looked at me and shook his head. He mentioned I should get my affairs in order. My heart was so bad I'd likely only have *6 months to live*. He continued the conversation, but I no longer listened. I thanked him for his time and left his office.

I cried the entire two-hour highway drive back to the mountains of Whistler

I couldn't go home to my housemates. I wasn't ready to share my diagnosis. Eventually, they would have to know my diagnosis because if anything happened to me, they would need to call for an ambulance. Instead, I drove to my GP's office, a lovely older Irish doctor, and waited until he finished with his patients so he could speak with me.

If you believe in angels, this doctor was my angel. He listened to everything I had to say. He knew what was wrong with me and was the first to diagnose my condition. He had also received the test results from my Cardiologist. He was so kind. He also had the wisdom that comes with forty years of practicing medicine. His words would change my life.

"Lynda, I had a female patient who had an incurable disease about twenty years ago."

I waited. I couldn't look the doctor in the eye. I was afraid I'd have a complete breakdown. I was so sad and scared.

"She cured herself."

I looked up and saw he was smiling. From one Irishman to another and a woman who did believe in miracles, I understood what he was saying to me. *It was up to my Higher Power and me.*

And that's why I wrote **LOVE the Beat Goes On**. I knew I would get flak for the book and the story. The YouTube videos I put up would get hate mail. I understand all of it. When your doctor says you're incurable, or your mom is dying, or there is nothing more that can be done, you lash out at anyone and anything contrary to your situation. It's not that the hate mail is addressed to me. It's the anger and frustration of those who haven't been able to heal. We all have loved ones that we don't want to lose but feel hopeless and frustrated because we can't find the answers to their healing.

Even today, fifteen years later, I googled Idiopathic Dilated Cardiomyopathy. Here's what it says:

Is there a cure for cardiomyopathy? **There is no cure for cardiomyopathy**. However, you can control the condition or slow its progression.

I'm not sure why this is still the case as I no longer have Dilated Cardiomyopathy. It's been gone for all these years. But I won't argue with Wikipedia! I also have no idea why I was chosen to live a normal life. I took my Irish doctor's advice and made the decision to do many unorthodox things that weren't mainstream like they are now. Reiki was one.

And then in desperation after months of no progress whatsoever, I made the decision to fly to Sedona, Arizona to work with a Shaman. I share that story in my first memoir. I think my openness to anything that might work was why I turned to a healer. Is he the reason why the Cardiomyopathy is completely gone from my body? Was it a healing? Or a re-alignment from the powerful energy vortexes that might control the beats of my heart? I have no idea. But I can tell you that I am so very grateful for every single day that I'm alive.

Sometimes I think I was meant to begin my writing journey so I could share my thoughts with you. The world keeps getting bigger or smaller. It depends on how you look at it. We can open the internet and be in Paris, Istanbul, Mexico City, Ottawa, New Delhi, Bali, Mecca—or anywhere else we wish to research in our browsers. News is international and sensational. There is no limit to the amount of pain, anger, war, death, sadness, and sometimes joy that we can find the moment we go online. When I was a child, after the eleven pm news, the stations stopped operations. Technology has taken over our lives. With the introduction of smartphones, there is nowhere to hide. I can't imagine that this will ever change. It's therefore up to us to monitor how much negative information we allow into our lives. And in my case, into my heart.

When I get scared about life in general, and we all do, I remember that I've been incredibly grateful for every extra second I'm alive. When I gave birth to my first son, he was so comfortable inside of me that he wasn't going to come out! The doctors induced me and I ended up with an emergency cesarean. I cried because I was in so much pain. I vaguely remember a nurse yelling at me to stop complaining! My ex tells me the medical staff came out of the emergency room worried. They couldn't stop the bleeding. They told my husband he should prepare himself for the worst.

My memory is vague after that. All I know is that I could not hold my son for the first twenty-four hours after his birth. I didn't have the strength, and I was in and out of consciousness. I spent a week in the hospital. But I got through it. I do remember the doctor told me not to risk another pregnancy. I don't think he realized who he was advising. I wanted my boy to have a sibling. I waited nine months, then took fertility drugs a second time, and had baby boy. I knew what to expect this time.

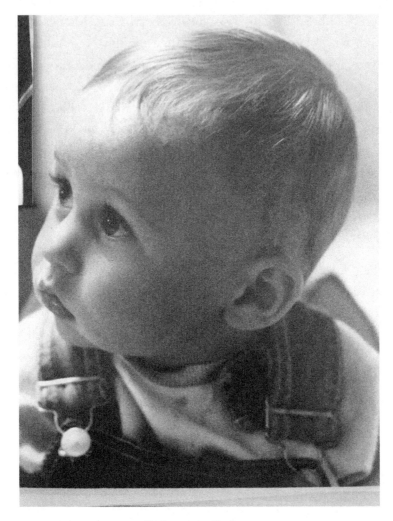

Zachary, my firstborn

I don't know why I feel compelled to share the story of my heart— again. Maybe I've held too many things inside of me my whole life. It could also be that I realized that all the emotional pain life had thrown at me had created my "swollen" heart—a physically "dilated heart." Or it could be that because I dealt with people as a profession made me aware that so many will tell a stranger their stories because they need to feel a kinship with someone who understands them. And that person is not always a family member or partner. Through the years I worked with people and listened to their problems. I found that we can relate when I'm authentic and vulnerable. And it's also cathartic to share your fears so that others know they are not alone. When I wrote my first memoir, <u>LOVE The Beat Goes On</u>, it was my time to release everything I'd held inside. But it would be several years before I published the story and shared my heart with the world.

My contract was extended in Whistler for another season. I felt fine, but it was time to go home to Mexico. I missed the sunshine and the lovely beaches of Puerto Vallarta. I could live a more relaxed, less pressured life, and I felt good there. Around 2010 I told a person I admired very much that I had begun to write the story of my healed heart. Her response to me was: *what if your miracle doesn't take?* I know she meant well, but I was paralyzed with fear and insecurity. What if I was merely in reprieve? By the time my story was published, I might be dead!

So, I put my book on hold indefinitely. And, then an event occurred five years later that changed everything for me.

6

THE ENEMY WITHIN

In 2015 a very famous motivational guru died: Dr. Wayne Dyer. I followed his teachings, read his books, and idolized that man. Not long after he passed away, I was peacefully asleep in my bed in Mexico when I was awakened suddenly by a very recognizable voice.

"Are you ready yet?" I sat up in bed and laughed out loud.

You can think what you want, but I've always believed that there is another world, an afterlife, voices that may guide us, and angels. After all, some being—I hesitate to put any kind of title—decides when it's time for us to go, right? So, I can't say I was surprised that I heard *that* voice, Dr. Dyer! It was time to get my act together, leave my ego and fear behind, and share my journey. There were people who needed to hear my story. And they will find my book.

I finally published the first edition and received kudos and negative comments. I accepted both. I understood the anger and helplessness many felt because they couldn't help a loved one with a similar diagnosis. After all, I'd been given 6 months to live. I survived. I get the anger, the frustration, and the heartbreak. When I did my YouTube videos, I knew I would be judged. Still, I answered every question. And if you believe in destiny, you know that even if we do everything right, eventually we all die.

It's seven years since I published <u>LOVE The Beat Goes On</u>, and I still get messages. I'm not trained in medicine, nor am I a therapist. I'm just a human who did a series of things that helped to heal my broken heart. Recently I received a message from someone diagnosed with the same dilated heart. She asked me to share what I did. Something made me dig deeper into who she was; easy to do on social media. I found a recent photo of her. She was much younger than me and at least fifty pounds overweight. How can I tell someone that her weight combined with Cardiomyopathy will kill her? That really must be done by her Cardiologist. Our hearts have a difficult enough job. The least we can do is take some responsibility for the emotional and physical abuse we put on our hearts. I knew most of my heart issues had been brought on by emotional drama/trauma. So that's where my work had to begin. I responded to her, of course, and suggested that she do whatever her doctor told her to do. It was the best advice I could offer. Maybe I had jumped to conclusions. There might be some medical reason she was so overweight. Either way, my heart goes out to her. I don't know her personally. But I hope she is comforted to know someone else has survived this disease.

Now, fifteen years later since my "6 months to live" diagnosis, I'm at work in my favorite coffee shop in Istanbul, Türkiye, writing this story for you. I've been in Türkiye since 2019 so I have a cardiologist who runs tests but tells me all is well. *Come back next year.* I have some permanent damage that does not affect my day-to-day living, nor do I need medication. I do take something for high blood pressure. My pressure is normal, but I take the meds every day. I can remember my mom saying that inside she still feels thirty-five. I'm with you, Mom! But I must face the fact I'm in my 70s, and I *should* have something wrong with this sleek, sexy operating machine even if I feel perfectly normal!

So, what do you do when the world has gone mad?

At first, the pandemic was an anomaly—I use that word for lack of a better word to describe an event none of us have experienced before. Life becomes overwhelming. Fear overtakes everything we do. In the early days, I continued to write on my sun-filled patio. I completed three books, The Istanbul Conspiracy and The Istanbul Heist in my Code Raven Series; and <u>Café Confidential</u>, a second memoir. And I was confident that no matter what the media was saying, in March of 2020, this pandemic would continue for at least six months. It turns out my prediction would be wrong. We are into the summer of 2022, and there are no new variants. We are finally mask-free in Türkiye; tourism is back. Life is moving along. I choose to ignore the whispers of further breakouts around the world. My psyche cannot handle it.

This type of fear had only affected small segments of the population in the past. When AIDS was first identified, the gay community panicked. And for a long time, that was all anyone talked about when sex came up in a conversation. But this insidious disease, Covid-19, has killed millions of people around the globe. We've all learned to accept some type of *new normal.* Still, we fear this pandemic may never truly leave us. Or if it does, will it be replaced by something deadlier? And as I review this part of my story, a variant (Omicron) has come and gone in 2022.

Unfortunately, we have learned how to live with the threat of dying. Some of us are doing better than others.

When I was young, we worried about a nuclear bomb. People built air-raid shelters. Thankfully, in Canada, we never had to use them. But it's almost impossible to protect yourself from a mutating Covid-19. There are all kinds of theories on how it began. Was it really released on purpose by some insane scientist? Will we ever know the truth? And even if we did, can we ever trust anyone's "truth" in today's world? We've all become scientific experts. We don't even believe in the efficacy of the vaccines.

Maybe this is our WWII. Some of us are fearful. Others not at all. Wherever you live in the world, imagine you are in Nazi Germany or elsewhere in Europe where bomb shelters existed. You are on constant alert to the possibility of death. Or worse, you are Jewish, and on any day, you and your family could be rounded up and taken to internment camps. You will be branded with a number and eventually led to die in the gas chambers.

My older brother was born before Dad went to fight in the WWII war. I was a post-war baby. I never really talked to my mom about her life during those times. All I know is she had her sisters, and cousins around her in the time of war. So even though we lived in Canada, there were more than likely some hardships. But it's not the same as hearing air-raid sirens and a life in constant fear of bombs. When Dad came home from the war, my older brother had never met him. And suddenly, a stranger was telling this little guy what to do. It must have been difficult for both. The war must have left its mark on my dad. But how would I know? I never knew this pre-war man. A post-war, hard-drinking, non-communicative man was the only father I ever had.

I don't remember affection. Neither the kind a husband and wife show for each other nor the kind a parent shows a child. It's strange because my mother was Irish, and the Irish are known for their joy and warmth. I only became a hugger when I moved to Mexico. The people are warm and friendly. It was awkward at first. I had to accept that this is the culture of Mexican people. But now I understand. I wasn't used to the closeness that comes with a kiss on the cheek or arms around me. Now I can say I'm much more demonstrative. The warmth of the Mexican people taught me to accept affection and give the same back. And now it's different yet again in Türkiye. I notice women often walk arm in arm. I find that so awkward. And yet the other day, while I walked through slush and rain, the woman I was with took my arm, and we gave each additional physical support. This might sound like a weird conversation to have with you. But as I age, I want to better understand myself, and when I do, I can change the things that I know will enrich my life. I'm a work in progress. Even though I'm in the last quarter of my life, it's never too late to learn how to give and receive love.

Some days I would like to blame my parents for the lack of connection to my extended family. We were constantly moving. That was military life during those years. I also feel like there is nowhere I call home. It never bothered me until this past year. I remember the day the conversation started with one of my close family members and the conclusion that led to my emotional dis-ease. But I won't go into it today. I'm still working through the hurt it did to my emotions. At the end of the day, maybe I'm searching for a place to call home. And that's why I keep that one suitcase packed ready to move on.

I often think of a wedding picture from my first marriage. The photographer asked my father to kiss the bride. It's a very awkward photo. It's as if neither of us knew how to respond to the request. But it doesn't surprise me because I don't remember an affectionate father. Could it be me? Could I have imagined all this? Maybe, when I'm all grown up, I will see the past in a different way. But right now, it's the only life I've lived. I know what you're thinking! I should go for therapy. You're right. I've tried it, but it doesn't seem to work for me. My therapist says it takes commitment and time. I've dropped it for now.

I know my stream of consciousness can be annoying at times. Maybe you can relate. I often think all this baggage was the cause of my swollen, enlarged heart. So other than to share it with you, I don't dwell on my past. But I know one thing. If I continue with these thoughts, I'm going to cry.

7

BARRIER BUSTING BOOMERS

I come from a generation of barrier-busting baby boomers. We have taken all those preconceived notions of what life and aging are all about and turned them on end. I never thought of myself that way until I hit my 50s. Mid-life crisis? Not really. My entire life has been action/crisis/reaction. Why should my 50's, 60's, and 70's be any different?

Today I'm working in one of my writing cafés—Starbucks, Findikli in Istanbul. Someone asked me recently why I sit at a Starbucks when I could be at a Turkish coffee shop. It's simple, really. It's a touch of familiarity. Also, the culture of Starbucks worldwide is a place to chat with friends, text, and often get some work done on your computer. No one looks at me sideways if I'm here for a few hours, writing, feeding the cats, and socializing with new friends who speak English!

I saw this on FB the other day. Our group, Lynda's Raven Army, can all relate.

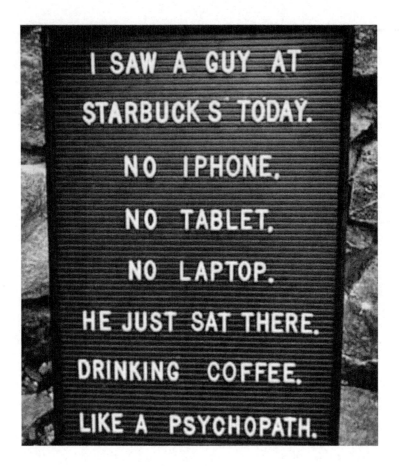

I SAW A GUY AT STARBUCK'S TODAY. NO IPHONE, NO TABLET, NO LAPTOP. HE JUST SAT THERE, DRINKING COFFEE, LIKE A PSYCHOPATH.

A few months ago. I had a brief conversation with a very stylish-looking group of Russian girls in their 20s. They had questions about an Istanbul landmark and assumed I was a local. I don't think I look Turkish. I'm obviously not a religious Muslim because my head is not covered. And the pink and purple streaks in my hair are in sharp contrast to the Turkish women my age in Istanbul. But I realized that I could be mistaken for a trendy local not out of place in my neighborhood in Istanbul.

It's been almost three years since I began my travels and eventually settled in this part of Türkiye. The waiters at the café on the waterfront nod and smile when I show up. The shopkeepers greet me warmly even though we've never been introduced, and we don't speak each other's language. I think they read my energy. They like it, and they forgive me for not learning their language. In any case, we manage to get by.

I went from living in a modern condo in a Mexican coastal tourist town of 18,000 people to Istanbul, a population somewhere around 17 million! That's quite a culture shock for me. However, when I liquidated my life in Mexico in 2019, I'd pictured a small studio loft somewhere in the world where I could create, maybe paint, read, discover new cultures, and of course, write. I found what I imagined in my mind. But I never dreamt it would be in a Muslim country in the Middle East in the middle of a worldwide pandemic. And as I edit this book, we are also in the middle of a Russia/Ukraine war!

And how did I end up in Istanbul, you ask? Life hinges on a couple of seconds you never see coming.

In 2019 when I decided I was ready for a break from Mexico, I had no idea what I would do. I had three published books of poetry and a memoir on healing from a 6-months-to-live diagnosis. I also wrote four romantic suspense novels. And I had begun to write my Code Raven spy series. So, I decided I could write anywhere. I sold my condo, and I purchased a series of one-way tickets. I thought I might end up in Bali. I could live cheaply, do photography, and write.

I've recently revealed that some Raven series characters are based on people who've come into my life. Their work is the kind that can never be written about as long as they are alive. I never knew their real names. But one of them died—at least I was told he died.

My instincts say it was a matter *of life or death*. I think my friend chose to disappear and fake death.

The first few stories in my Raven series were novellas. I would write one novella or maybe two. But then the characters took on a life of their own in my mind. I fabricated backgrounds and added more characters to my teams. As my imagination grew and my curiosity pushed me deeper into the issues in our world today, I found myself immersed in my imagination. I created a fictional group of ex-Navy SEALs and Special Ops, a strong female lead, and added characters who showed up on the pages of my stories without an invitation! I recently came across files I'd printed from internet conversations I'd had online in the early 2008/9. Those emails and texts led to the creation of the Raven Group. It wasn't easy *reliving* those memories. And in the end, I decided to trash all of them. But there is no doubt that those emotional relationships led to my immense curiosity about the rest of the world.

The initial novellas became so popular with my group of readers that I went on to write full-length novels and published them on Amazon. I wove in current events and created stories around the group. My imagination took over, and I became the scribe. I have nine stories in the Code Raven series, all available on Amazon. It's rather interesting that when I began writing this series, long before my journey in 2019, many of the locations where I set my stories were in the Middle East. Most of the countries I had never imagined I would ever visit. And Türkiye was not one of them. But the last two books, The Istanbul Conspiracy and The Istanbul Heist, are set in this mysterious city. And my imagination is waiting for me to complete this manuscript so I can find out what the Raven team is up to next!

There are places to see, cultures to discover, and people I'm destined to meet. I've always had an incredible imagination. When I write my fictional stories, I think of my father. He was an avid reader and communicator with international like-minded individuals, each on their ham radios. I think he would have been proud of this series. Despite some of my current challenges, I consider myself very lucky to be able to follow my passions in life and work.

When I sit at my cafes watching people, I imagine the lives they lead. I wonder about the countries they come from and what it would be like to have a conversation with these complete strangers. While I was having lunch at a new café in Galataport, a woman came up to me and introduced herself. She said she had seen me around the area, and she had recently moved here from Iran. We lunched and you can imagine that I asked her many questions. This city is filled with tourists this year, especially from the Arab world. There's always been a lot of Russian tourists in Turkey, but I'm not sure if that's the case right now.

Türkiye also hosts over five million Syrian refugees. We think a couple of million are in Istanbul. Most are not in my part of town, and many are younger and totally assimilated into the Turkish world. But I would like to hear their stories, especially since I wrote about the Assad regime in one of my first Raven books. There is a backlash amongst the Turks to the Syrian presence. Apparently as refugees, many services that Turks pay for are free for Syrians. And there's resentment and employment issues that have surfaced due to their presence.

Türkiye is not quite the melting pot of the US or Canada. But the US seems to be challenged by white nationalists and racism. In the last decade, the USA has changed. The headlines yesterday stated that *$106 Million* were *funneled into Islamophobic groups in the US*. I wonder if the culture in Canada was anti-everyone during the last century when my great-grandparents came from Ireland and the Protestant part of the family from Scotland. I doubt it, or they wouldn't have come to Canada or stayed.

But there is no question that people in the more 'stable' countries are concerned about immigration and the job loss created by the influx of immigrants. It's the same here in Türkiye. People of many cultures and several religions inhabit this city. Türkiye has an agreement with Europe to stop the flow of refugees and be the final destination. Türkiye has a monetary interest in doing so, as well. However, I read that many are going back now as the conditions have changed in Syria. War, refugees, and immigration all over the world is complicated.

One of the things that shocked me was the push-back of refugees by Greece. The Turkish papers report daily how many refugees are rescued in the ocean trying to reach Greece. The Greek Coast Guard block them, and Türkiye takes them in. In the middle of winter—the Greek Coast guard was accused of throwing three refugees in the water. One died, and the other two were rescued by Türkiye. During the winter, nineteen refugees were refused entry to Greece and were found frozen to death along the border between Greece and Türkiye. That incident is being disputed by Greece, of course. But who knows what is real when it comes to the news today?

It's so sad. But you can't dwell on it. We can only hope that the world will become more compassionate toward those unfortunates from poor and war-torn countries. I know I've always been a dreamer. But do you think one day we can place in positions of power human beings who are more heart-centered instead of angry and vindictive warmongers? Are we asking for too much during our lifetime?

The world is seriously screwed up. If you go to a site that shows the different news headlines, it's laughable. The distortion is different from paper to paper even in the Western world. News has become like reading one of my novels. You never know what's fact and what is fiction.

Türkiye is facing its own financial crisis right now. I won't discuss it. If you're curious, do the research. I'm not a financial analyst, and I will not hazard a guess regarding the devaluation of the Turkish Lira. Who suffers the most during times like this? The average worker and family. They are simply trying to make a living, feed their children, and save for a better future. It makes me so sad.

We are the barrier-busting boomers. Shouldn't we be able to do a better job running the world?

The Old Istanbul

The new, Istanbul

8

WANDER(LUST)

In early 2019 before any of us heard rumors of a worldwide pandemic, I decided to liquidate my life in Mexico. I knew I was giving up a great career, but I could always go back. I could even work in other tourist destinations around the globe if I so desired. I sold everything I owned and packed one suitcase. I bought a series of one-way tickets with no return destination. I had lots of options. I would figure out what I would do for the next part of my life when my tickets ran out.

I had a rough idea of where I wanted to travel, so first, I visited my son and grandson in Paris. I've told you about this in CAFÉ CONFIDENTIAL. If you haven't read that memoir yet, you will love my insights and the drama that seems to follow me wherever I go. I've also learned a lot since I wrote that memoir and I researched to understand many of the things I witnessed as I visited foreign countries.

One of the joys of travel is the surprises you encounter and the people you meet. But in reality, "I traveled the world to find myself." If I told you I'm shy, would you believe me? I spent a lifetime in sales. I met new people and lived in several countries. And still, I think I'm hesitant to speak to strangers. But I'm getting better! When you travel solo around the globe, there is no room for "shy."

I stopped in Dallas to see a Muslim man from Jordan I had met on an airplane. Yes, you read that correctly. We talked all night long on the flight when I met him. The conversation was very revealing for me. I had never heard the words "Islam is beautiful" before. Khaled opened my mind about his faith, and we became friends. After my stop in Dallas, I headed to France.

Paris wasn't a new city to me. I'd been there a few times during my fashion career and for my son's wedding. I was also fortunate enough to be there for the birth of my grandson, Felix. But everywhere else on my itinerary would be a totally new experience.

My journey would take me to visit my friend Himanish in New Delhi, India, a country that has its own caste system issues. Himanish and I met online. He's a book critic, and I read one of his reviews of my work. That's how we connected. He works in the financial sector, so he's my go-to techie when my computer starts speaking to me in a language I don't understand. We became fast friends and talked every single day for months.

Himanish came into my life to inspire me to be the best writer I could be. He encouraged me to write more books. He loved my work. So, of course, I would have to immortalize him in my Code Raven spy series! He even gave me the approval to use his name! I knew that we would meet in New Delhi. It turned out that we would have less time together than either of us would have liked. But I believe that everything happens exactly the way it's supposed to for a reason. We might not be able to see it at the time, but if we keep an open mind, we will find out why in the future.

I had a unique experience that stands out in my mind until this day. If you are ever in New Delhi, please visit here.

The Gurudwara Bangla Sahib, a Sikh Temple
One of Delhi's most famous destinations is this majestic shrine. It runs 24×7 and feeds 100K daily! It is dedicated to the eighth Sikh guru, Guru Har Krishan. Built by prominent Sikh General Sardar Bhagel Singh in 1783, it has a considerable body of water around it and beautiful carvings in the domes. The architectural marvel stands tall in central Delhi, close to Delhi's most famous church and Hanuman temple.

When I took off my sandals, and my bare feet hit the centuries-old marble floors tears flooded my eyes. There is no explanation for how overwhelmed my heart felt. My guide pictured above, took my hand and whispered, "It's okay. Many feel this way in this holy place." Organizations talk about the good they do, but I had never experienced the outpouring of love that I experienced here.

I knew that whatever this holy woman would share with me would be truthful and profound.

This temple is open twenty-four hours a day. And its purpose is to feed the poor or the needy for free. I can't even begin to imagine what the pandemic has done to the already impoverished people worldwide. Through the centuries, despite war and famine, this temple has remained open. Since the pandemic began in 2020, over four dozen men have kept this Sikh temple operating and continue to feed over 100,000 people daily!

That's about ten times more than usual. I know this holy place will be a memory that will warm my heart forever. Any one of these Asian Indian cities needed more time than I had allotted to see the incredible culture each offers. I would usually walk the streets and absorb the culture of a city. But my advice in India is to use a guide. You will see more, and you won't risk getting lost in places with safety challenges.

I have always lived my life directly from the heart. So, I had to visit the Taj Mahal, a symbol of LOVE—the word that defines my actions and reactions in life. It's magnificent.

The Taj Mahal

Taj Mahal, India

I was totally unprepared for the level of security in the Middle East and India. New Delhi has experienced terrorism, as have most of the parts of the world I would visit. Police barriers were placed for almost half a mile in front of the government buildings. They were staggered across the wide-open promenade leading to the stately structures. It took me a few minutes to understand their purpose. And then I got it. A truck or automobile driven by a suicide bomber would be stopped before the bomb could detonate and cause thousands of deaths. The same barriers were placed in front of the mosques around Sultanahmet, the number one tourist attraction in Istanbul, Türkiye. Each of these significant areas had already been attacked in the past by terrorists.

Security Barriers everywhere near government buildings in New Delhi.

In Mexico, where I'd lived for the last twenty years, these horrors didn't happen. You read about the danger of the drug cartels, but they stay in their own territories and fight amongst themselves. We never saw terrorism in sleepy Puerto Vallarta. However, from what I've read during the winter of 2021//2, things are changing on both the East and West Coasts of Mexico. The drug cartels are fighting for territory. Tourists and locals need to be more cautious.

But I don't even know how to explain terrorism in the Middle and the Far East. I was so inexperienced in traveling to these parts of the world that I'd never even thought of how conflict might affect my journey. I was very fortunate. Nothing untoward occurred during my travels. But now, security to avoid terrorism has become a fact of life in almost all parts of the world.

I've written about terrorism in my Raven Group series. But I've only researched the areas where most refugees are from, Syria and Afghanistan. I wrote The Istanbul Conspiracy while living here in Istanbul, So I dug deeper. I quickly understood that the prevention of terrorism is the way of life in so many major cities today.

We can't go into a shopping center or public building without opening bags and going through a metal detector here in Türkiye. And in the past two years, we've added bar-coded health IDs for vaccination and tracking Covid cases. We need to show this as well. This world has become a very challenging place. People accept all of this as the 'new normal.' Even with these security issues, I still believe that we should not let any of this stop us from seeing the world.

I hardly had time to visit with my friend Himanish, see a few intriguing parts of New Delhi, and visit the Taj Mahal. Then I was off to Goa, India, where I would relax on a fabulous beach. I was *Glamping,* five-star camping! *I didn't have a door I could lock.* It was an experience I enjoyed, but I must say, it's not for everyone.

Goa, India

9

BIG LOVE

After Goa, India, Chris, my travel planner, suggested two nights in Istanbul. He said it could be added to my ticket at no extra cost. Then I would travel to Israel, Singapore, Bangkok, and Krabi, Thailand. But before we talk about that, I have a confession to make. I've been blessed with good health my entire life. Sure, I had the odd broken bone, emergency Caesarean births, and a 'should' be fatal heart condition, but I've been strong and healthy for 99.9% of my life. I don't remember the last time I had alcohol. I never smoked nor did drugs. But while I flew from Paris to New Delhi, it suddenly hit me. I do have one *minor flaw*.

I fall quickly.

I'm addicted to love!

A few days after my time in New Delhi, I was sitting under a palapa in Goa, India thinking about a man I care about in New Delhi and a relationship that I knew could never be more than a lifelong friendship. If I don't write this story from my heart, my truth, you will feel my words are false. There's no cure for my *love* addiction—it's simply a part of me, like the freckles on my face and the extra ten pounds my body has insisted on holding onto my entire life.

Some people never discover why they exist. But I have finally accepted myself. Love and *being in love* are the essence of who I am. Before I explain—although it will seem insane to those who have never heard the siren call—promise not to judge me. If my story leaves you shaking your head, I can accept that. I write of these things to help me understand myself. And I write for those who yearn for the same self-love that has protected me my entire life. Here I am now, in the second half of my life. I've sold everything I have and I'm living out of my suitcase. I have tickets from France to India, Türkiye, Israel, Malaysia, Indonesia, and finally, the last plane ticket drops me in Thailand! From there, I had no idea where I would live or land. I know I've been telling myself it will be Bali. But as they say, "while a woman plans, God laughs!"

Eventually, it turned out I would let my heart lead the way.

I'm on the ultimate quest for love, even if I never recognized it before. Only this time, I'm determined to put my love of self at the forefront. If you wonder about my familial connections, I only have myself to blame for the lack of connection that has separated me from those I love over the years. If I could explain it to myself, I would share it with you. But I don't have the answers. And sometimes, it's best not to go into a negative space when you cannot change the past. You can only hope it will all work out in the future.

While we planned the stages of my *Eat Pray Write/Love* journey, my travel guide said to me, "For the same amount on your ticket,

I can add a two-day layover in Istanbul." My first response was, "Where is Istanbul?" It's not that I'm uneducated. I remembered the Ottoman Empire from my studies in high school a very long time ago. But Türkiye was not a country on my must-see list.

Little did I know that on a cold sunny morning at the beginning of March 2019, my life would hinge on a few seconds when I looked into the smiling eyes of a young Istanbul Turk.

"Hi, my name is Yunus Emre."

Hagia Sofia Mosque, Sultanahmet, Istanbul, Türkiye

The historic and the modern Istanbul, Türkiye

Vendors near the Blue Mosque, Sultanahmet, Istanbul

By now, I think you understand that I'm both impulsive and a hopeless romantic. I've lived my entire life with one enduring principle: *I will follow my heart wherever it leads me.*

I knew nothing of Türkiye or Istanbul. I had vague memories from high school that the Ottoman Empire comprised many countries. I found the city fascinating—what little I could see in those short few days. But I was on the trip of a lifetime. Nothing would get in the way of my journey. After two days and fun-filled nights with the charming but far too young Yunus Emre, I said goodbye to Istanbul and continued with my travels.

Next, I would journey to Israel, both Jerusalem and Tel Aviv. I've covered many of these locations in <u>CAFÉ CONFIDENTIAL</u>. But now, I've had so much more time to reflect. And a lot has happened, including the research I have done. For example, I learned more about the Muslim/Jewish conflict. At the time of my trip, I didn't know the details of the occupation of Palestine.

I've never been a history buff. My father was a math and science genius. He was into communications with people worldwide long before we had the abilities we have today. He and my older brother were what we would label "the brainiacs" in the family. My mother was brilliant too. I'm a woman of many talents, but memory is not one of them. My knowledge of the Middle East conflict was vague at best. Since I was neither born Jewish nor Muslim, it had not affected my life. Nor was any of this ever taught in the Catholic High Schools I attended.

Here's what Wikipedia has to say.

The Land of Israel, also known as the Holy Land or Palestine, is the birthplace of the Jewish people. It's where the final form of the Hebrew Bible is thought to have been compiled. And it's the birthplace of Judaism and Christianity. **It contains sacred sites for many Abrahamic religions, including Judaism, Samaritanism, Christianity, Islam, Druze, and the Bahá'í Faith.** The region has come under the sway of various empires and, as a result, has historically hosted a wide variety of ethnic groups. The adoption of Christianity by the Greco-Roman world under the Roman Empire in the 4th century led to a Christian majority in the Levant. This remained largely unchallenged until the Arab conquest of the region that followed the rise of Islam in the 7th century. It persisted for another six centuries as Muslim rule was consolidated despite various Christian military expeditions; by the end of the Crusader period in 1291, the Levant had shifted towards a Muslim majority. By the 13th century, Arabic had become the region's clear dominant language. It was individually first a part of the Mamluk Sultanate and, after 1516, a Syria-region province of the Ottoman Empire. **Muslim rule over the Land of Israel ended during World War I, with the successful Sinai and Palestine campaign that lead to the partition of the Ottoman Empire and the establishment of British rule.**

The late 19th century saw the widespread consolidation of a Jewish nationalist movement known as Zionism, as part of which Aliyah (Jewish return to the Land of Israel from the diaspora) increased. **In World War I, the British government publicly committed to creating a Jewish homeland and was granted a Mandate for Palestine by the League of Nations for this purpose.** Arab nationalism, in opposition, also claimed rights over the former Ottoman territories and sought to prevent Jewish migration into British Palestine, leading to growing Arab–Jewish tensions. **Jewish sovereign independence was nonetheless achieved in 1948 with the Israeli Declaration of Independence, which coincided with the 1948 Arab–Israeli War, the exodus of Arabs from Israel, the exodus of Jews from Muslim states, and the beginning of the Arab–Israeli conflict.** Today, approximately 43 percent of the global Jewish population resides in Israel, and comprises the largest Jewish community in the world.

In 1979, the Egypt–Israel peace treaty was signed, based on the Camp David Accords. In 1993, Israel signed the Oslo I Accord with the Palestine Liberation Organization, followed by the establishment of the Palestinian National Authority. In 1994, the Israel–Jordan peace treaty was signed. Despite efforts to finalize the peace agreement, the conflict continues to play a major role in Israeli and international political, social, and economic life.

This helps explain how I stayed in the old city of Jerusalem in a seven-hundred-year-old apartment (rented through Air BnB) owned by an Arab Christian man. I thought Israel was a country created for the Jews after the atrocities of the Nazi regime in WWII.

It only made sense that the home of the Jews would be in what we call the Holy Lands. I had learned little about the Muslim faith, but I knew about Catholicism. I had a good education and attended three years of university, yet I assumed everyone that lived in Israel was Jewish! I had no idea of the conflict that created the country. It never occurred to me that Israel was annexed from the land of another country. And to do that, you must basically redistribute land already occupied by another culture or religion. But this is what happens during war times. The best way to sum it up is to say: *what a mess!*

My Airbnb host met me at the airport. The drive was long enough for us to get to know each other. I found my conversation with Michael fascinated me. He, and his best friend, who came along for the ride, invited me to Bethlehem on the West Bank for dinner. I really should have posted that on FB. "I'm busy this evening. *Going to Bethlehem in Israel for dinner with my two new Arab Christian friends.*" Arab Christians? I thought all Arabs were Muslim.

The culture shock of my first twenty-four hours in Israel was tremendous. But it also gave me an up-close and personal opportunity to talk with my newfound friends about what was going on in Israel/Palestine.

Slowly my mind began its own journey. I questioned everything. I simply couldn't understand that humanity still acted like cavemen after thousands of years. Fair or unfair. They still refuse to get along.

Check out this map I found on the internet. If you can make any sense out of it, fantastic!

Religion Wiki Map

Justified or not, men want to wage war and take over territories like children on a playground. The only difference is that people worldwide are being murdered and displaced every day due to the insatiable antics of war-mongering individuals. I've been working on this book for several months now. It's long enough to witness the buildup of armaments on the borders of Ukraine. As of today, the aggressive actions of Russia don't match the political message of the head of Russia. The world has become such a small place. We are so interconnected today. Why waste all this money and energy on war? There will be a tremendous loss of life and millions of displaced people. And unfortunately, my instincts were right on. Those warships on the Bosphorus returned to Russia to wage war.

But the significant difference in a war today is communications. You can't hide your actions. The aggression in Ukraine, the murder of innocent people, and the destruction of cities—are unjustifiable. It really makes you wonder if unlimited power not only corrupts but moves into the area of insanity. What is the point to bomb a city, demolish everything, displace the people who live in that country, all for a piece of dirt? There's no answer for my current conversation with myself—and believe me, I will always keep my political thoughts to myself.

There are so many good things that we should focus on. Ultimately, don't we all want a good life? We need a place we can call home, jobs, food, clothes, healthcare, family, something to believe in, and peace. Why can't all the money spent on war/or defense budgets instead be spent on food, education, and job creation? Then the worlds' displaced people could have a life. I tend to ramble, but I can see you nod your heads. I know you agree.

With the developments in space and long-range weaponry, the world keeps getting smaller and smaller. We certainly learned this when we saw how quickly the pandemic spread. I began to label my 2019 trip the #WeAreAllOne journey. I doubt it's a philosophy that is likely to happen in my lifetime. But with the advance in technology, and the ability to eradicate another's country, if humanity is to survive, it must happen in yours.

Entrance Gate to where I stayed in Jerusalem, Israel. Ancient stone hallways filled with merchandise for sale lead you to the Wailing Wall or Western Wall.

Check, please! Culture shock in Israel.

Tourists or locals? Muslims or Nuns? Jerusalem, Israel

After a few days in Jerusalem, I went to Tel Aviv. It was cold and windy, so I was not particularly impressed. I didn't know anyone and had made no efforts to connect. I stayed in an Air BnB high-rise apartment. The home was lovely, even if I did hear a bomb drop a few days before my birthday!

As I walked along the oceanfront, I fell in love with all the street art. It's indeed a creative city. I would like to go back in the summertime and give it a second chance to impress me. Of course, that would have to assume there are no new outbreaks of Covid and no new wars in the Middle East!

Tel Aviv Street Art everywhere!

Creative Tel Aviv Artwork

Street Art Tel Aviv

Tel Aviv alley art!

Colorful and insightful Tel Aviv, Israel

I neglected to mention that before I married the father of my two boys, I converted to Judaism. This comes from a Catholic girl who went to the convent to become a nun. I wanted to have children. I felt they needed a religion. And it couldn't be Catholicism because forty years ago, I would have been an outcast as a divorcee. I couldn't teach my boys principles I wasn't sure held true for me. It would be hypocritical. I suppose you might say my journey as a *once Catholic nun-now Jewish woman* was conflicted. I know I've managed to confuse you too, but when you read **LOVE, The Beat Goes On**, my first memoir, you will see where I was coming from.

It was recently the 80th anniversary of Holocaust Remembrance Day. I wouldn't usually allow myself to read reports of such an insane negative time. I was disgusted by anything I read about the hatred of the Jews by the Nazis. I guess I truly am a "Pollyanna." I can't picture what kind of evil it would take to systematically murder six million Jews. For a moment, forget who ordered the destruction of a race of people. But what about all those who assisted in the crime. Wouldn't you have to be insane? In the eighties, I personally witnessed the stamped number on the arm of two old Holocaust survivors. To brand a human being for any reason is evil. Extermination camps, gas chambers, mass burial sites—I could never have lived in those times. But then communications were different. The world at large didn't know everything that was going on. I can't imagine myself in the country of Germany because of its' past. It's sad to blame an entire country for the Holocaust. And that may be the most painful sentence I have ever written.

I have too much time on my hands since I left my 9-5 job and transitioned into travel, and writing full time. I am my father's daughter. He would use his Ham radio to contact the world in the 1950s. I use my computer. But aren't we supposed to learn from the past? So why do we continue to fight wars? And they do seem to be divided by religion. Why would we determine the worth of an individual or culture by the faith they follow? In a way, there are things I've read that I wish I hadn't. For example, there's the current treatment of India's "untouchable" caste. It's painful and frightening to see what human beings can do to other human beings for no reason other than where they were born.

Since I began to edit this memoir, Putin has continued to attack Ukraine.

Communications have come a long way. You can't hide your evil today. There are no words to describe how I feel about this. Here I am at my Starbucks "office," drinking coffee and listening to cool music, and people a few thousand miles away are suffering unspeakable pain and fear. I try to keep calm and remain normal during this surreal time. I've got the doctor visits for anxiety to show for it. It's not easy feeling the collective negative energy of the world. And that means I must avoid the news for days, if not weeks. And as I edit this memoir, I have managed to avoid the news another day. It's simply too sad to follow what is going on around the globe.

I will never understand war. I think it's simply part of the male DNA to fight. Don't send me hate mail for that comment, but soldiers for centuries have been male. Maybe if we replaced every world leader, including those in the Muslim countries, with women, the world might have a chance at survival. Instead of fighting over land, why can't we ensure the world's population has food, medicine, a home, and a job. The money spent on so many contentious egotistical battles and power-hungry bull-crap is depressing. It seems the world will never change. Each generation is greedier than the next.

I shouldn't allow myself to go down this rabbit hole. I know most of you understand what I'm saying, but maybe not *why* I'm bringing it up. The bottom line is while I was in Jerusalem, I saw Muslims praying outside the Al Aqsa Mosque and Orthodox Jews bowing in prayer at the Western Wall. Both, at the same time. So, no matter what we call our Higher Power, whether it's Allah or God, it's the same Being. So, again I say to myself: *why can't we all get along?* When will the human race understand #WeAreAllOne?

Next stop BANGKOK

A boat trip at night was the perfect opportunity to
photograph the beauty of this city.

Krabi, Thailand

Muslim Ladies at the Beach in Thailand

Krabi, Thailand, working on my freckles!

My final ticket was to Thailand, a perfect place to gather my thoughts and relax on the beach. I'd spent over fifty years working in my career in design, manufacturing, retailing, and resort sales. I'd earned this break and my idea of retirement. Bali beckoned. There was only one small problem. Every day I awakened to a message from Yunus Emre: *Come back to Istanbul.* And finally, when my last ticket ran out on the 8th of April 2019, I received this message:

I know I am poor, but I have a big love to give.

Instead of a one way ticket to Bali, I purchased a ticket to return to Istanbul. I've been here ever since. Little did we know what life would throw our way over the next couple of years.

Krabi Beach Thailand

10

ME TOO

I can't remember the name or face of my first attempted rapist. I was sixteen (during the '60s) when a girlfriend asked me if I'd join her and her boyfriend on a double date. The friend was twenty-two. It was a bit old for me at that time, but it would only be a date. I don't remember what we did or where we went. But somehow, during the evening, we ended up at an outdoor park in Ottawa we called the "Overlook."

We went for a walk, and the couples became separated. Before I knew it, my date had me pinned down on a hill in a remote park area late at night. I can still feel the weight of his body holding me down. I was a virgin and hardly knew this man. I panicked but came up with a believable 'time-of-the-month' excuse. I managed to talk my way out of the situation by promising another date the following week. I was freaked out and scared, but I remained outwardly calm. I never told anyone. He was a twenty-two-year-old off-duty policeman! If I reported it, who would have believed me?

To understand the present, sometimes, we must revisit the past. Many things helped define the woman I've become. But all these events, minor and significant, are part of what forms us. And sometimes, to understand ourselves, we must pull out the old anger and hurts and let it all go. I've managed to forget most of the ugly events in my life. But when I need them, the memories come back. You might wonder why I would bury these thoughts. But when you feel helpless, there is no point to hold on to thoughts of adverse events.

My mother had her own "Me too" moment entirely different than mine. Her generation married and were expected to be housewives. The average woman could have a job until she got engaged. Before my mother married in late 1939, she worked in a yarn factory. She loved her life and her independence.

When I was a young girl, I vaguely recall my mom sharing her story of dating Dad. I do know he was not the love of her life. My father was the son of well-off protestant store owners, and my mom was a country farm girl. I don't know much about their courtship. But my mother was a very religious Catholic girl, and morals were not what they are today.

But my father was in love, and he pursued her. One day Dad showed up with a diamond ring. She intimated to me that she was never passionately in love, and when dad gave her that ring, she didn't want to put it on. But she said she would think about it and took the tiny diamond and placed it in a drawer in her home. I vaguely recall mom talking about an Italian man named Sal. I don't know if my mother dated him or simply had a crush on him. He may have been her first love. In any case, I think he was the reason my mother was not excited about the proposal from my father.

But as the story goes, Mom had a despised female supervisor at the yarn factory. For some reason, she tried to make Mom's life miserable. One morning, the supervisor waltzed into work, announced she was engaged, and flashed her diamond ring. That evening, my mom took the ring Dad gave her out of her drawer and placed it on her finger. The following day, she walked into the factory and announced, "Me too."

I don't think I ever understood love or romance on a deep level during my younger years. But *Me Too* took on a whole different meaning for today's generation with the testimony of Christine Blasey Ford against Supreme Court Justice nominee Bret Kavanaugh. It became a heated topic as women worldwide began to discuss how powerless so many of us felt over the years. But we know how ineffective her testimony was in preventing his placement on the Supreme Court. And now, he is part of a group that will legislate how much power a woman has over her own body.

Not much has changed in fifty years. I think it's likely that most women from my generation have experienced sexual harassment in the workplace. We never talked about it when I was younger because we felt helpless. And, of course, we would have been accused of "asking for it." These sexual attacks generally happen without a witness, so it's always a matter of 'he said' and 'she said.' Today we know that sexual harassment goes both ways. A small percentage of men have experienced the same pressures. But for some reason, we don't see it in the same way. Maybe that has to do with the fact that, for the most part, physically, a man is better able to defend himself. Not to say that men don't experience some form of harassment to keep their jobs. Unfortunately, it is still a man's world when it comes to equality. We quickly forgot the

"Me Too" movement. Those of us who had our untold stories buried them once more. In 2022 it looks like women's rights have been attacked once more. And with the conservative US Supreme Court, it seems like the country will go backward, not forward.

My philosophy has always been:
One, I bury bad things.
Two, I move on.

That simply means I believe that as we age, if we carry all those sad stories in our hearts, we have no room to find the kind of loving relationships we seek to fulfill us. But maybe I've been wrong. If I'd talked it all out throughout the years, I might have finally found the relationship with another, and with myself, that would sustain me until my death. Instead, I kept my sadness buried deep in my heart until my physical heart finally had enough and broke down in 2008. I'm fortunate to be alive to share my story today.

11

POWER(LESS)

As a child, I often sketched clothes. My mother taught me to sew when I was very young. When I was eleven, I had my first job at the local beauty salon. I would wash hair. I could use that money to buy fabric and make my own clothes. I loved design and fashion. I still do. I never thought of it as a career at that time. I didn't really know it existed. In my generation, our background and upbringing dictated that we would become nurses, teachers, or social workers. But fashion was my passion. I can still picture a turquoise velvet shift dress and white boucle coat that I made from pattens purchased at Eaton's. It was all I remember of my high school graduation over fifty years ago! That outfit would still be in style today!

I was always creative. All design fascinated me even though I was not formally trained. I looked for a job in that industry when I moved from small-town Ottawa to the big city of Toronto after my first six-month marriage was annulled. While I searched for work, I met a man who was several years older than me. He had a sales office and represented companies from the Canadian fashion capital at the time, Montreal. I became his showroom model. Sexual banter and harassment went with the job.

After a period of time, Sonny and I became lovers. We managed to put together enough money to start our own business. I'm a smart girl. I did well in school and took college courses even though I never obtained a degree. We were partners and eventually opened one store. I can still picture the "contractor" who helped build that store. We were halfway through the build when he broke his ruler. We used a piece of string instead to measure when and where the shelves should go! There might have been the odd shelf or rack that wasn't even! It's strange how I carry that memory with me. Those were exhilarating and creative times. I loved my work. Eventually, one store turned into several, and we had a factory where I designed and had the clothes manufactured.

Sonny had the credibility and background in the industry to get the money we needed from the banks to do our expansion. And, of course, as partners, I signed on to the debt. Eventually, we had a factory and ten retail stores. I thought it might be a good idea to protect my assets and my contribution to the business, so along the way, I married my 'partner.' He was not the love of my life. Instead, it was one more way to make sure I was protected financially.

There was only one problem. I had married an adrenaline addict. I had never been exposed to a gambler before. Sonny bet at the horse races and played the stock market. Basically, he bet on anything he could play the odds. I was this naïve Catholic school girl from a simple military family. I had no idea about horse races or gambling at the Crap tables in Las Vegas. It was all an exciting novelty for me. I got to dress up in glamorous Vegas evening wear and watch the high rollers lose thousands of dollars with the roll of dice. I never thought about where my husband was getting the money to bet on the horse races or play such high stakes at the casino. He was fifteen years older than me. I assumed he was successful financially when I met him. This naive optimist got carried away by a glamourous lifestyle I'd only seen in movies.

When it all fell apart, I was the one who blindly co-signed all the bank documents that were placed in front of me. After my business went bankrupt, I learned from the head store manager that my husband would take money from all the cash registers each day. In the early '70s, we didn't use computers. The store supervisor's job was to re-do the tapes that recorded the sales so they would mask what was missing and equal what was left in the till. She was afraid to say anything to me because she didn't want to lose her job. Instead, she lost it anyways because the wholesale and retail businesses had to close, and everyone was let go.

All the business books I'd read at the racetrack neglected to teach me anything about a lying, cheating gambling business partner. It's frightening to find yourself in bankruptcy. I approached a second divorce—even though my first marriage of six months had been annulled by the Catholic Church. I quickly lost my confidence in my ability to choose partners, both romantically and in business.

I had to make a new life all over again. I'd married a very controlling man who would never allow me to leave him. I had three years of college but no degree. The only experience I had was in fashion and most of that was learned on the job. My self-esteem was damaged, and I was embarrassed. But I had no time to wallow in self-pity. One thing I knew for sure, I was grateful for the birth control pill and the fact that I'd not had children in either relationship.

When I finally got up the nerve to escape that marriage, I literally had to disappear in the middle of the night. Over the years, I befriended a wonderful family in Montreal. The only talent I had was my experience in design and retail merchandising. I secretly called this family, and they said they would take me in. I picked a time when my husband was out of the home, packed one suitcase, and left. A few weeks later, my ex found out where I was located and where I worked. He tried to get me fired from a new job so I would come back to him. He wasn't successful. And now, between too much alcohol and food, he was a full-blown diabetic. He needed needles daily, and he was a good fifty pounds overweight. He really needed a nurse, not a wife or lover. Eventually, he gave up on me. I never saw nor heard from him again.

It's 2022. I don't look for pity or expect you to understand. My only hope is you will see that we all make mistakes, or what I call 'life lessons.' Some we think are the end of the world, or at the very least, we're embarrassed. But don't make yourself crazy. I promise you, life will go on.

As I write this memoir it's brough back many memories. I recently searched for this man on the internet. Whatever happened to Sonny? I hadn't spoken to him since I left him in the late 70s. It took a few tries. I only searched for a death notice. I knew he'd been married before me because he had two young teenage children. He had diabetes and physically abused his body with alcohol and food. The stress related to his addiction to gambling only made it worse. I knew he couldn't be alive. It turned out he remarried very soon after me. There was a mention of a widow, and a former wife, the mother of his two children. The date of his death was 1986. No cause was indicated.

After my split from Sonny in the late seventies, I talked myself into a buying job for a children's wear retail group. I had not been formally trained but I had talent and confidence. I didn't know the professional terminology, so I found a book and did a crash course in wholesale and retail buying. I was very good at picking styles that would sell, and I was successful at my job. I got my own apartment and finally felt safe. All was great for several months until my repulsive boss showed up at my apartment one night. He invited himself into my place on some business excuse and raped me. I couldn't fight him. Instead, I focused on the dandruff on the collar of his navy velvet jacket and waited for him to finish.

There was no point to report the rape. He could have spun the story to suit his narrative. Maybe he would say I'd offered sex to keep my job. I had no fashion school degree. The rape would have been his word against mine. He wasn't the first to take sex from me against my will, nor would he be the last. But in my own mental health interests, I had to let the episode go. Date rape or rape by a person you know is a challenge to prove. I did the only thing I could do. I never showed up to work the next day. Now I had to look for another job.

"Why did you leave your last job?"

"My boss raped me." *Right.* Go put that on your resume!

I wonder how many women of my generation have been raped by someone they knew. It's still going on today. I'm not the only one who never reported it. I didn't even go to a doctor. I was on the pill, so what was the point?

Around the same time, I thought it might be a good idea to get a divorce from my gambler husband. He certainly wasn't going to do it. And who knew if he was falsifying my signature to obtain loans for his new debts.

I found a divorce lawyer. Hie listened to my story of woe. He seemed to think this job would require help. He brought his partner/brother in to hear my pathetic story about my failed business and compulsive-gambler-husband. They decided that my body should be part of their payment for doing my divorce. I have a vague memory of the sexual harassment, but I can't even remember if I went along with it or not. Imagine what they would have said if I reported them to the Canadian Bar Association? "She offered her body for a better fee deal." *Wink, wink.* I buried that event in the same graveyard as many that had happened before.

I developed a thick skin and became an expert at moving on in my life. I only share this because I want you to know other women have gone through the same things that you might be encountering today. Women are sexually harassed and raped all over the world. We still blame the victim even if we don't say it aloud. But women are strong. We learn from our experiences, grow, and hopefully, move on. I'm not saying that what I did was the right way for you to handle these types of events in your life. I believe it was the right thing for me at that time.

Over the years, I chose to bury events like that because they hurt me more emotionally than physically, and there was no possibility of changing the outcome. If it's difficult to prove now, imagine what it would have been like in the '70s. It was his word over mine. I was sleeping with a man to keep a job, or I was part of the fee to lower the cost of my divorce. Either way, it would have been a waste of time.

I never like to revisit the negative aspects of my past because there is absolutely no benefit in remembering the hurt or drama for me. I only share this with you, so you will know you are not alone. Many women have gone through similar experiences. As women have become more powerful in the business world, men have gone through sexual harassment too. There have been challenges for as long as women have been in the workforce. The adjectives used to describe us are very different than those used for our male counterparts. Despite all that, women rock and rule in their careers. When a woman is secure in who she is, she is unstoppable.

The world is changing in many ways. I love that a man can be the caregiver at home, and his wife can build her career. I also admire women who can take time off from their careers to have their babies and stay home with them as they grow. We also must accept that we are not superwomen. Some things will get left undone. We can't do it all.

It's cathartic to write and release these thoughts. And as I sit here at my favorite writing spot in Istanbul, let that be a part of my legacy. I will remind myself that although I'm going through a rough emotional time right now, I've still lived through a worldwide pandemic in a country where I don't speak the language. And I'm finally able to write again and continue to share these thoughts with you.

When the #MeToo movement began, I thought it might be a good time to write my story. I would have to dig into the past and unwrap several carefully buried episodes. I might have gone way back to my childhood. I had an uncle I've long since forgotten who made six-year-old me feel uncomfortable when he would insist that I sit on his lap. My sister did reveal not too long ago that this uncle had married a widowed woman with two young daughters. Apparently, they got divorced a few years later. No one knew why they divorced. I kept my opinion to myself.

Maybe I'm a dreamer, but I believe that one of my secrets to living well into my '70s is the ability to *let that go!* I choose to fill my heart space with love: self-love, love of the things I do, the people I meet, and my friends and family. If you spend too much time in the past, you have no room to allow the light and love of the present to come into your life.

My advice is to write all those hurtful, nasty events down. Use separate pieces of paper for each one. They've already taken up more space than they deserve in your heart and head. Have a burning ceremony. Let those limited despicable memories go up in smoke. And take some advice from *Alice in Wonderland*. **Believe in the magic**. Trust me when I say that once you've let it all go, you will have room in your heart and soul to thrive rather than merely to survive.

12

I NEVER PROMISED
YOU A ROSE GARDEN.

I lived a settled life in the '80s and early '90s. I married a fun-loving young Jewish man from Montreal, and we had two boys together. For a short time, I sold real estate in Montreal. We eventually moved out to Western Canada and the mountains of British Columbia. The boys could ski and snowboard, and I could sell the dream. I'm vague on dates, and they aren't that important to the narrative. But for many years, I lived my idea of stability.

When you look at your life, you must accept that if you are doomed to repeat a pattern that you run away from your partners, the common denominator in the narrative is *you*. I know that I've spent a lifetime in a search for the perfect relationship. It's amusing that I've been watching the Indian Matchmaker series on Netflix. I get it. How about finding out if you share values with a guy before you allow the physical attraction to distract you? If there was ever a woman who could use a Matchmaker, it's me! (Now, this is a perfect example of how my post-Covid mind jumps subjects and comes to conclusions in one paragraph.)

I don't think I set out to make the same mistakes repeatedly, but marriage is something I've never been able to figure out. I've had three partners. Each one did last longer than the last. So, I might have learned something. Or maybe I'm still trying to learn to love myself.

The father of my children has recently returned to my life after an absence of twenty years. We didn't have much to do with each other for years after I left home, but we did have two sons together and spent more than twenty years married. Now that both boys are well into adulthood, we would occasionally have conversations online about our kids, but that was it. Now we seem to have become friends again. He still lives in the mountains where our boys grew up.

He was looking at photos of our life together. He asked me, "What went wrong?" I thought about it for a minute, then left him a message. The first words that came into my mind were: "I felt like I had three kids instead of two. I think I got tired of the responsibility."

He never responded.

I didn't have to explain.

However, we still chat.

A few lovers have come and gone. I thought I found *Mr. Right* several years ago. In the early 2000s, I was on a dating app. I met *many* men. Some were worth a conversation, others not so much. I can see all my singles nodding heads in agreement. And if there was no photo, I ignored the approach.

This man somehow captured my attention yet obscured his looks. If I remember correctly, he showed a photo of a sailing boat, a small yacht, in the PNW of the USA. By this point, I was divorced from the father of my children. I had come out of another relationship in Mexico. I was looking for someone I could relate to—maybe more 'age-appropriate.' I had more flexibility. Work was going well, and I thought it might be time for a grown-up-rest-of-my-life love. I don't know what it is with me. I think I've been doomed to choose intriguing and impossible men. Dr. G. was no exception.

Is he the one that got away? Maybe. But I also believe in fate. I'd finally grown enough to understand myself and what I wanted and needed in a partner. He was closer to my age. That's a big deal for me because very young men are attracted to me, and we know there is no future there! I saw him off and on for a couple of years. And then he had a health crisis that he would not explain. He disappeared from my life. I grieved him for a long time. I still hear from him every year or so.

Why are all these memories coming to me now? I thought they were buried so well. But my new MacBook, upgraded MAC system, and Steve Jobs had another idea in mind. When I finally uploaded the *macOS Monterey*, I was shocked. Every email exchanged between Dr. G and me from the time we began our relationship was in my current messenger file. I don't know where I had them hidden before. But when 'the one that got away stares you in the face, it's like a raging out-of-control fire you drive by but must slow down to watch regardless of the danger. And so began hours while I re-read and re-lived one of the hopeful yet drama-filled times in my life.

Dr. G was a patriot. Due to inventions and investments, he was also a genius and an extremely wealthy man. He was funny and compassionate. Domineering and very loving. Frustrating and a pain in the butt—not literally. With time I learned that his wife had died from an incurable disease. And because he was a scientist and a doctor and brilliant, he blamed himself. Why? Because he couldn't find the cure before she died. He refused to date or have any relationships after she passed on. But his teenage daughter didn't want her dad to live the rest of his life alone, and she put him on the dating app. And as the story was eventually revealed to me, I was chosen with her approval.

I was mesmerized by the emails we'd sent back and forth. Our lives, our laughter, and a lot of poetry danced off my computer screen. As I read our old correspondence, my mind was drawn to that time. My heart was assaulted with a depth of emotions I'd so carefully buried under layers of impenetrable cement. We would meet in Canada or the US, always last-minute plans that sometimes changed if there was anything that felt 'off.'

It's one thing to live in this type of clandestine relationship. It was necessary to read between the lines to understand what was said and what could never be written down. But when I read the bulk of emails together, I truly began to grasp this brilliant scientist, a man who had dedicated his life to protecting his country—even if it meant the loss of his life. And then, one day, everything changed.

Almost twelve years have passed. I still will not write the details of what transpired. But this is likely why I've remained single. To deal with that time in my life, I immortalized and fabricated a life for him in one of my book series. I dwell on him when I start a new book in that genre. The subject of Lynda's love life—or the one that got away—is on hold indefinitely.

13

WHERE IS ISTANBUL?

I don't like drama and refuse to live in an unhappy household. It goes back to my teenage years and the tension I witnessed in a home dominated by an alcoholic father. I will not blame anyone for the choices I made in my life. I'm simply trying to make sense of my actions/reactions and my lack of tolerance for conflict in my personal/emotional relationships.

Once I was on my own, I only had myself to blame if I was unhappy or disappointed with anything. I've been single now for many, many years. Poor planning possibly. Did I see myself single at this stage of my life? I guess I always allowed my heart to fall into relationships that didn't seem to have a future. I don't know. I never looked this far forward. I was too busy living in the present and keeping it together. But I understand and accept that the one common denominator in all my relationships is me.

Maybe we can't have it all. I've been blessed with successful careers. After many years in fashion, I found the travel industry. I've been forcing people to take vacations for thirty years and loved every moment. If I wasn't talking about travel and selling the dream to others, I lived that dream. Not everyone can make a career in world-class ski resorts in Canada and fabulous ocean properties in Puerto Vallarta, Mexico.

It's been a fascinating journey, if at times a lonely one. But I must shout out to the friends I've made in sales over the years. You have inspired me, maddened me, driven me crazy, refocused me, and loved me. And for that, I'm forever grateful! Many of you are still in my life on social media, and in many ways, some of you are my adopted family. I hope you feel the same.

In 2019, I liquidated my life in Mexico and retired from my sales job. I decided there was much more to see than the beaches of Mexico. I was tired of inappropriate boyfriends and online relationships. Looking backward, I can see that now. I understand myself enough to know that I engaged in these relationships, so I knew from the beginning that there would never be a 'future.' Maybe that's how I tried to protect my bruised and broken emotional heart. It seemed that relationship stability and long-term love were not meant to be a part of my destiny. The closest I got to a white picket fence was a magnificent ski chalet in Whistler, BC, with a husband and two sons. But that was not meant to be forever either. I'm not complaining. After all, I knew what I was getting into. And I was always the one who walked away. You can't move forward if you are always looking backward. Grow, forgive yourself, learn from your experiences, and move on.

In 2015 I published my first memoir, <u>LOVE The Beat Goes On</u>. I *loved* writing my story, even the painful parts. All the things I went through, my physically and emotionally broken heart, were meant to be shared with those who needed help on their own journey. I grew so much after I was given 6 months to live in

2008. My experiences and the techniques I learned I still use now. And as often as I can, I share these things with others and the world. Words are powerful. If I can help even one person navigate their life, health, or relationships, it's worth the bleeding I need to do to revisit some of the painful events in my life.

My first book award: <u>Lie to Me: an exposé on sex for money</u>

By the beginning of 2019, I had published three books of poetry, four romantic suspense novels, and my first memoir. After I sold my condo and all my belongings. I decided that everything of value would fit in one suitcase. The rest would be in my Prada knapsack, my memory and my heart.

When I made this monumental decision in my life, I'm sure my friends and coworkers thought I was crazy. Maybe I was running away—again. But instead, I thought it was time to learn more about the big world out there. I don't remember how I found Chris, my travel planner, but he offered his professional services to coordinate my trip. I gave him many destinations that were of interest to me. Two musts were Paris, to visit my son and his family, and New Delhi to say hi to my latest chat buddy, Himanish. I also wanted to visit Israel. Chris booked my trip, and my last destination was Krabi, Thailand. I had no return tickets. Even though I'd lived in Mexico off and on for over twenty years, the Army Brat in me had never really found a place I'd call home. From Thailand, I would begin a new life somewhere. In my mind, I thought it might be Bali. I was now semi-retired, and I was ready to spend my days reading, writing, and doing photography.

I don't know what I was expecting, but it turned out I would spend my 72nd birthday in Israel listening to a bomb explode in Tel Aviv. I thought it was a bold move when I left my ex in Canada in the early 2000s and moved to Mexico. But my #WeAreAllOne journey in 2019 was on another level entirely. Maybe I would end up writing in paradise. I was only a plane ride from my family and friends. I wrote about this fantastic experience in CAFÉ CONFIDENTIAL and shared photos with you earlier in the book.

I never thought about the dangers of travel by myself to these foreign countries. I've always been a curious girl. I smile as I write that. I'm brave for the big things but a wuss for the small stuff. I got all my travel inoculations, organized my finances, made copies of anything I thought I might need, and packed my suitcase. How did I fit an entire life into one bag? I still haven't decided if a lack of possessions is a good thing or a bad thing. But the most valuable things we have in life are the love of those we are close to and our memories; and they will remain in our hearts forever.

I know it seems I have lived my life backwards. Or maybe it took a lifetime for me to have the courage to do what so many young people do during their college years. I was too busy first with the novitiate, and next I built businesses; and of course I lived with inappropriate men. I did learn a lot of relationship lessons even though I might be doomed to repeat them.

I was far too serious about my life to backpack through Europe when I was twenty. I had not yet developed the type of confidence and curiosity required to travel the world independently. Yes, I'm living my life backward. But that's what life is about. We all develop our wings at different times in our lives. 2019 was my time to fly, literally and figuratively.

"For the same price on your ticket, I will add two nights in Istanbul." Chris texted me.
"Where's Istanbul?" I responded.
"It's in Türkiye! Everyone loves Istanbul. It's filled with history."
"Okay, why not."

He forgot to tell me how dangerous the 'boys of Sultanahmet' could be!

You reach an age and stage in life, and you think you have yourself all figured out. But you absolutely do not! What's the spark, that connection that pulls two souls together?

Sometimes I wish I could look at life more logically. But it's never been how I made my decisions nor chose my partners. I think the heart in you reaches out and touches the heart in me. I don't think about the outer shell, the age, or the feasibility of acting on the connection. I don't think about the consequences. What I didn't see coming at the time was at the end of my epic journey, my heart would lead the way.

It's three years now that I've been sheltering, healing, and writing in Istanbul. We hope we have come out on the other side of a worldwide pandemic. But we don't know for sure. Whatever the future holds, I think my mother would agree with me when I say I am Destiny's Daughter.

Karaköy unique shops, and my other Starbucks' "office" nearby.

Famous fish restaurants under the Galata bridge. Istanbul at night

Ferry port, on the Bosphorus Strait, old mosques in the background

Nighttime near the new Galataport Cruise Ship Terminal, Istanbul

14

MARRIAGE IN THE 21ST CENTURY

When I blog online, my area of expertise is photography and writing. Baby Boomers between the ages of 57-75 and how we are busting myths and traveling solo are also my passion. Boomers have pushed the envelope from the time we were born. We have a lot of firsts in our lives. But the one that seems to have defined our generation is how we challenged the existing sexual mores. We were the proponents of free love in the 60s. Although we soon learned that nothing is free. Unwanted pregnancies led to the development of "the pill." With the sexual freedom of women, new confidence developed. Pregnancies could be controlled, so women could now choose long-term career goals. Women busted glass ceilings and initiated extramarital affairs—previously the domain of men. Unfortunately, divorce became mainstream. The stability of the family unit was threatened in ways we had never witnessed in our parents' generation. We evened out the playing field, but we also paid the price.

In my parent's generation, divorce was unthinkable. First, divorce was forbidden if you were Catholic, as was approximately twenty-five percent of the US population in the sixties. If you were a stay-at-home wife on an average-income family, it wasn't financially feasible to walk away from a bad marriage. The divorce rate in the late 1950s was somewhere around 3-6% depending on which website you check out. By 2014, the baby boomers were often on to 2nd marriages as the divorce rate had hit 22%. Each of the four kids has been divorced at least once in my own family. I read that statisticians say that up to 50% of first marriages will end in divorce! That's an ominous sign of the times. Have we become a society of fast food, throw-away diapers, and dissolvable first-time marriages? We are supposed to be more advanced than the generation before. But then school doesn't have 'relationships' on its roster of subjects to study in high school. Our mores are changing. It seems everyone you meet has been divorced at least once. I'm at the front end of the Baby Boomer generation. I'm comfortably single, financially speaking. But what will happen as more and more women face a lonely and financially unviable senior age and stage of life?

Do we have unrealistic expectations of our partners? Or is it simply that we married too young. Do you really know who you are and what you want in your 20s? I don't have the answers. All I know is what I see. We are a society—especially women—who will not tolerate the circumstances we witnessed with our parents. Happiness, equality, and immediate gratification have become our mantras. My parents stayed together for religious and financial reasons. When I look back, my father mellowed out eventually. And in the end, I believe my parents were happy or content with each other. Maybe they had it right. Who knows?

I've been fascinated by the diversity of Netflix offerings during this latest wave of Covid paranoia. I'm learning about East Indian culture, food, design, RuPaul—my sister's guilty pleasure—the housewives everywhere, and real estate worldwide. I could go on and on, but you get the idea. I've also learned the way different societies deal with marriage. So, back to divorce in the 21st century: what do you think of arranged marriages?

I watched several East Indian series on dating, how to find a mate, and arranged marriages. It's pretty fascinating. When I first met Himanish from New Delhi a few years ago, I had no idea how an Indian man and woman go about marriage. When he decided it was time for a serious relationship, he went on a "marriage website." That's right. A website dedicated to those whose sole intention is marriage. I investigated the process. I didn't know such a thing existed.

Thirty seems to be a turning point in people's lives. Or maybe there was pressure from his family. But when he also told me that his future partner would be moving into his family's home, I was surprised. I didn't ask any questions. I had no idea at the time that this was normal. The son stays at home, and the daughter-in-law comes to live with the family. I thought that might be a way to save money for a down payment on their own apartment or home. Now that I've been watching all these traditional Indian shows, I see that this is the custom, the culture. It certainly solves the problem of what will happen to your parents when they are old. It might also be the answer for young modern Indian women who wish to continue their careers. The mother-in-law can look after her grandchildren.

Then I watched another program on Indian matchmaking. It's an essential profession. The family has a great deal to say about the type of mate they see for their son or daughter. It also turns out that in many cases, the bachelor's mother oversees this process. She is the head of family matters and has a lot to say about who her son will marry. Yes, the son can accept or reject, but Mother will push to get a decision. It's fascinating when you think about it. Instead of judging partnerships strictly by your hormonal response to a smile, body, or eyes, you lead with the intellectual side of your attraction. And for a man, that means the decision is made with the big head, not the *little one*!

Another series I watched dealt with East Indian singles in the US who were more modern, living on their own, over thirty, and had not yet found a partner in life or love. Generally, these women or men were busy building a career and had only decided now to find a life partner. They also preferred to marry within their culture. So instead of swiping on Tinder, a professional Indian matchmaker is called in to do an assessment. That person might advise you on the areas of your life preventing you from finding happiness. More than likely, you need a makeover from the inside out. All of us can use that. If you are looking for an Indian mate after the age of thirty, you might be living on your own, possibly have a demanding career, and could be living outside India. These factors change the type of mate you might choose. I had no idea some Indian matchmakers specialize in this area, too.

The matchmaker studies the questionnaire you have filled out. Then she interviews you. If she feels you need to overcome a psychological obstacle, help is suggested. It's up to you to take her advice or not. Profiles are matched. Then you have a first date to see your level of interest. And take it from there. Couples get three dates chosen by the matchmaker. Then you decide which of the three you wish to meet for a second date and possibly a future. Your selected date has the option to accept to take the relationship further or not. Again, it was a really different look at the process of marriage. These will ultimately be love marriages. Someone who has no emotional involvement in the match can analyze the character and interests of each potential partner before the introduction and the attraction is determined. I would encourage anyone looking for a mate or with children of marriageable age to watch these shows. When I think back on my failed relationships, I can see how someone from the outside would look at my choices and know from the start that they would never survive.

When my friend Himanish found his mate, I liked to think I was part of the process. He was on a marriage dating site and contacted or spoke with various women he felt could be a match. I was in Istanbul at the tram station in Sultanahmet, chatting with him on my cell phone. I don't know how many women he had approached at that point. But Himanish is methodical in everything he does, so I can imagine that he went on his search with a vengeance once he made up his mind. At this point, he had not met The One.

We didn't waste time discussing the different women. But then he told me about the most recent one. She had given him her What's App number, and he was supposed to contact her at a specific time. Something happened, and he didn't call or text at the agreed time. When he did get around to it, she had deleted him! I started laughing. And without a photo or any further information, I said to Himanish, *she's the one!* And it turned out she was.

I was living in Istanbul when the marriage took place. I was invited to the wedding, but he did explain that the bride and groom sit apart from the guests, so I wouldn't know anyone there and I might not be that comfortable. Now that I've watched the Indian wedding shows on Netflix, I get it. Traditional Indian weddings are very different than anything a Canadian girl can imagine. The clothes, the dances, the foods, everything was so exotic. I would have been out of my element. So, I declined. But I've got my pictures. And I can see how happy they both were on their memorable day.

I've not met his wife, but I wonder if he ever told her my prediction!

15

BOOMER WISDOM

A few years ago, I discovered an online site named Quora. It's the largest Ask & Answer site in the world. For me Quora has become a place where the younger generation can ask the Baby Boomers questions. And anything related to writing or photography are the subjects that interest me the most. Everything is discussed. Experts drop in and give their point of view. Some Quorans only ask questions. I only answer questions. I had no idea that Quora paid members for questions! But I never saw the site as something I would use to generate income. I found it filled with knowledge and answers from those who have figured out how to get the job done. It might be how to run an author business or any other career or personal question you may have. If I was immersed in a writing project and needed a break, I would drop into Quora and answer questions.

I've got over four million views on Quora. I came to the site late for the party, but it's been fun. I'm open and willing to share my life experiences, and it seems many have been inspired or at least entertained by my antics. It turns out that the site is a great way to also talk about my two memoirs, <u>LOVE The Beat Goes On</u> and <u>CAFÉ CONFIDENTIAL</u>. Many fans and readers have come from that site and have joined us on FB at Lynda's Raven Army. Our Facebook site is a private group, so we can talk about anything we want, and we do.

When I answer a question on Quora on any subject related to my life or my work, I reference my memoirs. If the question is on how to write fiction, I refer to my Romantic Suspense, Contemporary Romance, or the Code Raven Series. Once I realized the power of over 600,000 views on an answer, what started out as a curiosity for me, a way to 'warm up' before working on my current project, became a way to reach fans who decide to purchase my books, as well. I'm self-published through Amazon, so I am my own publicist and promoter. It's a challenge to find a market for my books as I am neither famous nor infamous! It's only recently that I realized how important Quora can be to share my books.

As the population is aging, it makes sense that a trendy subject on Quora is Aging.

Here is my most viewed Quora question and answer to date. I answered this at the end of 2019.

How does aging play out past sixty? Did you notice things changed dramatically after sixty? What do you wish you'd known a decade earlier to help you prepare for it?

Someday I will get old. But as long as I'm not... Oh yes, my life did change dramatically after sixty! I'm a late bloomer and a baby boomer. Here's what happened to me after I turned fifty, then sixty, and now soon to be 73! (Now 75! yikes)

I improved my attitude and perfected my "I don't give a damn what you think about me!" I fully embraced my life, the love in my life, and who I am.

*I moved to Mexico (from Canada) twenty years ago because I was in love with a very young Mexican guy. We eventually split up. Dating someone much more youthful than you will toughen you up to **what people think!** I still had a lot to learn about the woman I was becoming.*

*When I hit 61, I was diagnosed with incurable heart disease and given 6 months to live! Instead of wallowing in self-pity (I tried that with my family but couldn't get any sympathy), I turned to the things that had sustained me my entire life. Faith, Reiki, Self-healing, Shamanism, and a positive attitude. Other than one co-worker—I managed a large sales entity—I kept my dis-ease to myself. When I published my story in 2015 on Amazon **LOVE The Beat Goes On**, I finally admitted my age. That was the year I turned 68.*

*Why did I finally accept my age? **I wanted to be an inspiration to young women: turning 30 or 40 or 50 or 60 is NOT the end of the world!** At this time, I felt my life was just beginning! Maybe I've been blessed. I feel exactly the same way I've felt my whole life, except I'm finally free—free of the self-limiting belief that there are things I cannot do.*

I was never an athlete, so I had nothing to miss in that area, and never very adventurous. But in the past year, I sold everything I had in preparation for retirement. I left my beloved Mexico to travel and find a new place to live. I spent my 72 birthday in Tel Aviv. I think I will celebrate my 73rd in Istanbul, where I'm currently settled but maybe not.

So I feel the most together I've ever been in my life. Yes, I'm blessed with good health. I try to do Yoga every day. Sure I take meds for high BP and heart (I no longer needed heart meds in 2021), but that's not WHO I am. I refuse to allow my mind to dwell in that place of "I'm getting old… and I'm sick, and woe is me!" I will not do it. I also have a young guy in my life—it's six months now. He says it's our destiny. Whatever it is, I'm having the best time of my life.

I write, do photography, blog, have fun on Quora and say the most outrageous things. I conveniently left out that time in my life when to serve as an inspiration for other young women on my 70th birthday, I finally admitted my age. **I got fired a week later.** *Yes, age had a lot to do with it. Why further invest in someone who will more than likely leave soon. So what. Maybe it was the Universe's way of saying get out. It's time to move on.*

I love life. I always remember my smiling grandpa, who went out to feed the cattle on the farm one day, returned for his afternoon nap, and never woke up. He was 93.

Do you think my mom is watching me from wherever souls go when the body dies? I hope she's smiling at my unconventional life. I know she would be proud of me.

Now wish me luck. It's my first winter in Istanbul, Türkiye—I bought a fuzzy jacket to hide under!

First winter in Istanbul 2019

Here's an update to that top-rated answer on Quora:

Update 2020! What a spring and summer it's been so far!! I have written another memoir you might enjoy. <u>CAFE CONFIDENTIAL</u>, *an unfiltered and intimate memoir. It's available on Amazon.*

A chance encounter with a young Muslim man on a flight to Paris, a friendship with a book critic in New Delhi, and a doomed love affair led a hopeless romantic to liquidate her life in Mexico and buy a series of one-way tickets with no return destination.

Find out what life can be like when a woman in the latter years of her life decides to let go of her past and fit all that she treasures into one suitcase.

So grab a cappuccino or herbal tea and join Lynda at Café Confidential. She will share her adventures and secrets as she travels to France, India, Israel, Malaysia, and Türkiye. Perhaps she can convince you that it's never too late to follow your dreams.

The population, in general, has a massive curiosity about a modern woman over 70. Who is she? What does she think? How does she feel about aging? After all, we are a generation that venerated youth. But I believe that I am the most confident I have ever been at this age and stage of my life. I have independence and enough funds to be relatively comfortable. It's the first time that I don't have a constant *dis-ease* about my job, career, finances, health, and love. I'm comfortable in Istanbul. And I refuse to angst about my future. After all, I worried about my career, future, money, children, and relationships my entire adult life. Don't you think I can chill for whatever years I have left?

The most significant portion of the world's population is Boomers. We are not our parents. We are aging in an entirely different world. We want to know what to expect. I hope my stories can shed some light on what can be if you are prepared to accept your age and stage in a way that celebrates your experiences. I like to think I'm a role model of different choices. And I'm not alone. If you go to **We Love Memoirs** on FaceBook, you will find like-minded individuals. Read their adventurous memoirs. Dream of the way life can be rather than living with fear and a false notion that life is over the year you retire from the business world. Single or married, you have a whole new life ahead of you.

I don't want to make light of health or financial issues that many faces at this stage and age. I simply want us to look at these years as the beginning of many opportunities that were not available to us in the past.

Here's my second most viewed answer on Quora. Again, you can see the curiosity of young and older people as they move towards this time in life.

What can you expect when you are over 70?

Would you believe me if I said I am the happiest I have ever been?

If you expect a response filled with regrets, NEXT! Let me share some secrets with you.

Has life been perfect? Far from it. I've been divorced three times— not my most outstanding achievement. I could write my own book on the #MeToo movement—but I won't because it will only dredge up past memories that would remind me of what it felt like to be powerless. And yes, I've had many hardships and disappointments. But what's in it for us to dwell on problems, or the past, hurts, and pain?

Here are some of my thoughts.

1. ***I feel good, even great***. *I see no difference between me now and me 30–40 years ago—except I'm definitely more content. (I accept my current on-going anxiety, but if that's all I have left over from Covid, I can fix this.)*

2. ***It takes a lifetime to understand yourself***. *It's an ongoing project to learn what's important and what we should and should not stress about.*

3. ***The most essential piece of the aging puzzle is self-love.***
   I know it sounds very new-age, but it's true. If you haven't figured out how to love yourself by 70, you might as well give it all up and move on to wherever we go when we die!

In 2008 I was given 6 months to live. *Those of you who follow my ramblings already know this about me. And thanks, by the way, for reading my memoir on Amazon, <u>LOVE The Beat Goes On</u>. The long and short of it was the doctors said I had an incurable heart condition. And everything I read about it said the same thing. These challenges in life are turning points. They really show you who you are and demand that you decide how you will live your life/diagnosis. Do you accept it? Do you get your affairs in order as my doctor suggested?*

I did many creative outside-the-box things because I'm here now! That will never preclude Divine intervention. It really wasn't my time to die. I think my outlook changed a lot during the next ten years. I've lived in Mexico off-and-on since 2002—I'm a Canadian. I made the decision to celebrate my 72nd year in 2019 traveling. I sold everything I had and lived out of a suitcase. I began in February in the US, then on to France, India, Israel, Türkiye, Malaysia, Indonesia, Thailand, and on. I don't know what I was thinking. I was now homeless! I could always go back to Mexico or on to another warm location where I could afford to retire and write full time. But during my two nights in Istanbul, I found someone who seemed to think that LOVE was something I needed and encouraged me to return to Istanbul.

I know, I should write another book! At least that's what my friends say. And I will when I finish writing book 7 in my Code Raven spy series!

I altered the above answer to bring it up to date, and I did write that memoir, <u>CAFÉ CONFIDENTIAL</u>. And finished the Istanbul Heist book 7 in my Code Raven Series.

This is another highly viewed answer with over three-hundred and sixty thousand views this year.

What is the single most underrated trait a person can have?

It's such a cliche. I know you will not read further than the second sentence.

But, as a woman approaching 75 years of age, I think I've earned the right to set you straight. **Attitude.** *And I don't mean to give attitude. It's so easy to become jaded about everything. Life will always be filled with setbacks, disappointments, lost love, divorces, problems with our children. I'm sure you can fill that negative list in a heartbeat.*

But the most critical yet underrated trait I've discovered is **positive thinking**. *We can permanently alter our focus to celebrate the good things. You know that there is always a way to put a positive spin on things no matter what life throws your way. Sure, it's easier to wallow in self-pity. But, if we can spin everything that doesn't go our way and look at it from a different angle, our lives will be so much richer.*

People are always tell me they can't believe my age. *I get it completely. It's not about beauty or having a fantastic body. It's about the smile in my eyes, the wonder I can still find in this incredible world. I find joy in the silliest things. But it keeps me young and filled with wonder.*

Try it. It's actually a fun way to approach life!

If you're curious, read my previous memoir, CAFÉ CONFIDENTIAL, and find out how a Canadian girl living in Mexico ended up in Istanbul, Türkiye!

16

CAN YOU FIND LOVE AFTER 70?

There are many questions I get asked that I don't answer on Quora. Why? Because they are usually followed by unwanted private messages. I don't have the time or desire to play online games with anyone. As we used to say: *Been there. Done that. And have a few emotional scars to show for it.*

Sex is one of those subjects. To have it or not is such a personal decision. If you are in a mature relationship, you know what I mean. Sometimes one partner wants it more than the other. But it's not a subject we can ignore. We're no longer kids. We don't want to leave our partners at this age and stage. This could be our last big love. It's unlikely I can say that for myself as my current partner is a much younger guy. Eventually, he will marry and have babies.

Over the years, I've wondered if we all have past lives. Did the two of us meet in another place, another decade, another country? I mean, what really happens to us when we die? Do we come back again? Was I a Turkish woman in another lifetime? Was Emre my husband? Or was I one of the Prophet's wives?

See how my mind can get away from me? I know that Emre and I met for a reason and a season. Who knows how long that time will be for us? When we first met in 2019—those fateful two nights I spent in Istanbul—I never thought I would come back. But I had spent the last several years without a relationship. A series of crazy insane events and men had come into my life. They turned out to be great inspiration for storylines in my Code Raven Series. But none were boyfriend or marriage candidates. It seemed that I was always going to be alone. And in one way, I'm still alone. I haven't lived with a man for twenty years.

But I envision I will know when the time is right to move on. As painful as it might be for one or both, I knew this going into my relationship. If I had to do it all over again, there is absolutely nothing I would do differently. Sometimes, I wish I could be that young woman who spends the rest of her life having babies and being loved by a man like Yunus Emre. But I accept that what we have found in each other is part of our destiny. We both needed what the other offered when we met. And when the time comes to let each other go, we will know.

If you have love and a relationship with a younger man, sex will be part of your attraction. If you want to have sex into your 70s, you must take care of yourself. Our bodies change. Listen to your doctor and do what he says. I'm still in good shape. I know what you're thinking! Don't laugh. I've always been ten pounds overweight!

I start my day with a shower, then I meditate. I enjoy Deepak Chopra's ten-minute meditation, but I will do more than one meditation when I feel the need. I do it outside on my patio, even in the cold or rain. I use an umbrella and sit on a sturdy patio chair

120

while I listen to my meditation on my computer or cell phone. I can watch the ferries on the Bosphorus or the snow that fell overnight in the park. It helps to clear any anxiety dreams from my mind.

Immediately after meditating, I do yoga. This year the choice is Adriene. If I've sat on my cute butt a lot the day before, I might do a neck, shoulder, and backstretch routine. And sometimes I will do another twenty minutes in the evening. Adriene has put together so many different focused, relatively easy practices for whatever is bothering you. She's also got workouts that are perfect for beginners or seniors.

I'm happy I'm back into these morning habits. I'd slacked off for a few months. The morning is the most challenging time of my day. I often wake with anxiety, and I need to move through the first couple of hours with focus. I fight it but when I need it, I take medication as well. I will add links to both Deepak and Adriene at the back of the book. Even 20 minutes of yoga will help you.

I also know how important it is to stay well-groomed. I would look after myself, I would see that as a sign of depression. My nails are polished, and I get my hair done with fun colors like pink and purple. I like that I've always been wild, trendy, and curious about everything around me. Practicing habits like taking care of my physical body and emotional health makes it easier to go through this anxiety. I refuse to give in to depression. So my gratitude list is endless!

rebelthriver   •••

rebel⚓
thriver

She was never quite ready.
But she was brave.
And the Universe listens to brave.

−Dr Rebecca Ray

My age and stage of life haven't changed my attitude. I try to see the upside in all things. I'm not good with negative people. I remember once my ex-husband was arguing with me over something, and he said: "Take the needle out of your arm." I was confused. I had no idea what he meant. Years later, I realized he equated my 'high' to an injection of drugs. My positive attitude drove him crazy.

I don't need recreational drugs to be happy. I will always look at life as if the glass is half full. I am grateful that I've never been addicted to drugs or alcohol. I'm content to live in the present moment no matter what problems I experience. I know that *wherever I go, I take myself with me.* If I'm going to travel with myself for the rest of my life, I'd rather be with a woman who was curious, and in love with life than a bitter old hag!

17

LIVING LIFE BACKWARDS

I know I misplaced the memo that stated, "do your exploring when you come out of college." I tend to live my life backward. When others have settled lives and are possibly preparing for a comfortable retirement in Florida, I'm off roaming around the world in search of new experiences.

Never in my wildest dreams did I imagine I would live in a Middle Eastern country. But I've always said, be careful what you focus on. When I began to write the Code Raven series, I researched different countries where I would set the action. Little did I know I would end up in Istanbul and base my last two novels, plus two memoirs, in this city.

So, what is it like to live in a Muslim country in the Middle East? First, a disclaimer. I live a comfortable middle-class life. I'm not in slum areas. I wouldn't walk outside alone at night, like in any large city. But in a city of 17 million (unofficial numbers due to the difficult-to-count Syrian refugee crisis), you can be certain dangerous places exist.

In my neighborhood, situated along the waterfront between many Historical parts of Istanbul, 98% of the language spoken is Turkish with some Arabic. But many do speak English, French, Italian, German, and more because of tourism. I'm never wholly frustrated. If anything, I'm annoyed with myself for a wasted three years when I could have learned Turkish. But I will make no excuses for my laziness. I use Google translate if I have internet, or somehow, I make it work. The staff at Starbucks are not all bilingual, but my favorite Barista is a lovely young girl, and she doesn't speak any English. She only knows the menu in English. We get by because our smiles and hearts speak the same language. And there's Google Translate on our phones!

I'm always respectful of my surroundings. Signs of affection in public rarely happen here in Istanbul. In my neighborhood which is younger and trendy, it's more common. You will see handholding. And you can see the love between a couple and their little ones. It's just that the culture is discreet. Lately I see more affection with younger couples. I'm not saying that Istanbul, Türkiye is like all Muslim countries. The country is supposed to be tolerant as Ataturk is the architect of the Republic of Türkiye and designed the country to be secular. However, a portion of the population would like Türkiye to be more conservative and become the leader of the Islamic world. I saw a notification of a Jewish celebration next week. President Erdogan makes a point to wish the Jewish people a happy holiday. I have not heard of any persecution of other religions. But then, if it was happening, it might not show up on news sites I have access to for several reasons.

If you visit Taksim, one of the most famous tourist shopping areas in this city, you will see beautifully restored Catholic churches.

The breakdown of religion depends on the statistics you read. The government says 99% of the population is Muslim. Wiki says 89.5% is Muslim, with the difference being agnostic or Christian and Jewish. People are free to practice whatever faith they want and wear whatever clothes they like. I see girls in short shorts in the summer and women wear leggings and crop tops. And then, of course, we see women in stylish hijabs that cover the head. Country women often wear headscarves in colorful patterns. And there are parts of the city that are more traditional where women wear burqas—the burqa covers the entire body. The garment is always black, and only the eyes show. Where I live, it's rare to see a burqa, and if I do, it's most likely worn by women who are tourists from Arab countries.

This past week, I was wandering in a classy store in a very upscale shopping center. A woman was wearing a burqa with only her eyes showing. She was purchasing a gorgeous sequined dress. It was modest but something anyone would love to own. I asked my friend: What's the story? So apparently, the burqa is only worn outside the home. Inside, anything goes. Then I remembered the Fabulous Lives of Bollywood Wives on Netflix and their trip to Doha. When the women removed their burqas, they were dressed both elegant and fashionable. And in Sex in the City 2, the wealthy Arab women revealed the latest Parisian styles under their burqas. This is all I knew about the Middle East. I didn't realize that all Arab/Muslim/Middle Eastern countries are different and impose various levels of observance.

Çamlıca Republic Mosque largest and newest opened March 2019

The founder of the Republic, Attaturk, wanted Türkiye to be secular. And that's part of the challenge for the Muslim religious right. It certainly makes people-watching very interesting. So is it a sign of where the world is moving towards? Could all religions one day live side by side? Maybe. But we all know that religion is a subject the world has fought wars over since the beginning of time. I don't really see that changing, certainly not in my lifetime.

The longer I live here, the more I recognize the differences. Istanbul comprises many people from the villages who have migrated to the cities for a better life. I've not really been to the totally traditional areas where women are covered in black with only the eyes visible. I know it exists. But it's not as common as I expected on the trams, hospitals, or the areas I frequent. However, I've been to the beaches and witnessed women in bathing suits and bikinis.

All women cover their heads in the mosque and are separated from the men for prayer. The women who cover their heads in this city wear modest stylish Western clothing. Their heads might be covered in any color, and their sweaters, jackets, pants, or long skirts are generally in the latest fashionable neutral shades. Elegant and modern. And as an aside, the Turkish people are beautiful.

Three young Muslim women at the park near my home. Bosphorus Strait

Religious dress of any kind in the Middle East will always be controversial in other parts of the world. I don't know why. I think politicians simply like to create disharmony. For years in the Western world, we've seen nuns fully covered in black, and we have no problems with that. Is the push back against the burqa or the hijab simply discrimination towards culture and religion?

I will quote an interesting article I came across today. This is an opinion from a young Muslim woman who lives in the US and is a writer. I looked for photos of her online and found some. She is not wearing a burqa or hijab, not in the images I saw. But she believes it should be a matter of choice.

Opinion: Wearing A Burqa Isn't Oppressive, The Ban is.
By Saumya Rastogi

"Naqiya Saifee, an 18-year-old girl from Surat in Gujarat, says she started wearing the "Rida" by her personal choice. "Some of my Muslim friends do not choose to wear it, and that's their decision," she says.

The veil has various forms in Islam, ranging from the 'hijab', 'niqab', 'burqa', 'chador', and 'Rida'. The Quranic verses talk about statements referring to veiling by the prophet's wives but do not make it clear whether it applies to all Muslim women.

An argument can be made that the West's decisions to ban burqas have less to do with liberation and more to do with islamophobia.

According to critics, the veil has been used as a patriarchal way of negating the male gaze and sexual desire toward female bodies. But many women who cover their heads or bodies say that it demonstrates their religious piety and submission to God.

However, covering the head or body does not only stand true for Islam. Jewish, Christian, and Hindu women have also covered their heads in different parts of the world at various times in history.

The question arises then, why have western countries banned the veil if women choose to wear it willingly."

As you already know, the burqa is a controversial topic. When I met my friend, Yunus, I didn't realize he came from a very religious family. She is completely covered with a burqa when she leaves home. She knows her youngest son has a "friend," and she asked him how I was doing. I thought it was kind of her to acknowledge me. And possibly it was her way of giving her approval to our friendship.

I ask a lot of questions. When you live in the Middle East in a country like Türkiye, it feels very European. You see the mix of cultures and the differences when visitors come from Arab countries. Every society, every country has both good and bad people in it. This is life. And there is no question that evil exists everywhere. Look no further than the insurrection in Washington on Jan. 6th. I am sure some people had good intentions but poor judgment. But most didn't. And we saw what happened in Afghanistan when the international forces pulled out.

Evil hidden behind religion or politics is not new in the world. It will always exist at all levels in all countries. I won't even go into the recent revelations of "thousands of pedophiles in the French Catholic Church." Do we really think this kind of thing only happened in France?

Oct. 5th, 2021 — An investigation into sexual abuse in the French Catholic Church has found that an estimated 216,000 children were victims of abuse by clergy.

My parent's generation didn't have the same access to information and news that we have today. If you want, you can be bombarded with bad news 24/7. I'm reminded of my dad in his workroom. He spoke with people all over the world. He would have loved the internet and our ability to communicate online. I think of him every day when I go to a news site. However, his interest was not in the negative events happening in the world. He spoke with like-minded techies and mathematicians and exchanged ideas.

Because I'm curious about world events, I check the news briefly. I also make sure to look for good and uplifting events. At night I will not watch any type of Netflix or Prime movie that is dark, violent, or disturbing. I'd rather watch food shows than have images of evil in my sleep. I always put "Good News" into my search options even though it's hard to find anything that's light or uplifting. I keep trying just the same. There are many things in this life over which we have no control. But we can choose what to watch, what to read, and where to focus our minds and hearts. I like to know what is going on globally, but I've learned a lot during this pandemic. I need to control the negativity I allow into my life. If I don't, I suffer and become anxious.

The internet can be like watching a train wreck over and over again.

Anxiety will sneak up on you. I know firsthand. Too much bad news will bring it up to the surface. But sometimes I'm compelled to read all of it, from all over the world.

I could use "Parental Controls."

18

AUTHENTICITY WILL SET YOU FREE

The sooner we accept ourselves, the more we can begin to live without self-doubts. Why would we compare our lives, accomplishments, and ourselves to others? We don't know what another has had to live through to get to the point where they can function.

These past several months have been an enormous challenge for me. I've been through so much in my life, so many disappointments that I've lost track of them. But I've always focused on the good and my world's positive aspects. A few things have happened that set me back and frightened me. You know how something can sneak up on you, and before you know it, you're caught up in an event or a life out of control?

First, the lockdown seemed to go on forever. It's not as if I'm social, but I'm out every day. Good or bad weather doesn't matter to me. I walk and surround myself with people. And I write at Starbucks! I know that's hard to imagine. Lots of action, coffee grinding, order taking, chatter. It's perfect. I have no problems tuning everything out to write. I never thought I needed people around me until the lockdown closed all contact with outsiders. At least I had my balcony and could watch the container ships navigate the Bosphorus Strait.

Container ships on the Bosphorus Strait as seen from my patio.

This city of seventeen million people was locked down for months, close to a year. I cheated. I admit it. After several weeks, I put on my coat and mask, grabbed my Canadian passport, and went outside. But I was afraid. In some ways, I'm shy. I hate to do something wrong and be reprimanded for it—it must be my Catholic school upbringing. I had my passport with me because a tourist didn't have to follow the country rules for Covid. Although I doubt there were many tourists in town because businesses were also closed. I don't like to break the law. I never want to be stopped or questioned. In any case, I would walk across the street and find a place to sit in the empty park. I love to watch the huge container ships on the Bosphorus Strait.

But I was nervous. I saw a few people out. They defied the lockdown rules. More than likely, they had appointments or necessary jobs. Finally, a traffic cop who used to watch me came over to talk to me. He smiled and was very polite. He asked me where I was from. His English wasn't good enough for a real conversation. I think he just wanted to know me. He nodded and left. I relaxed after that.

The lockdown went on forever. Emre would go to the grocery store for me. He would bring me a supply of bottled water and my diet cokes! And I spent most of my time on my patio even though it was winter. Months passed. Then in May of 2020, tragedy struck close to home. I didn't truly understand all the details at the time. But five people in Emre's family caught Covid. His father and mother were hospitalized. And that same night, his father died. I'd been exposed a few days before when Emre had visited me. I received daily phone calls from a doctor for two weeks—contact tracing. I was so lucky. I never got sick. There was no vaccine at that point, so I was very nervous. But the vaccines were on the way.

By then, all the anxiety had already caught up with me.

This was a whole new experience. I've been through a lot of events in my lifetime. But I've never felt so totally vulnerable and anxious. I went to my local pharmacist and told her how I was feeling. She gave me medication to take. After a couple of weeks, I couldn't really see any difference. Then I went to see my heart doctor for a checkup. He did his usual tests and told me everything was fine. I haven't needed any heart meds for a few years now. Everything was perfect. My pressure was good. He'd prescribed something to keep it relatively low. I told him how anxious I was feeling. He prescribed medication to lower anxiety. After a few weeks, I continued to feel the same nervousness. The worst were my nights. I hated my vivid dreams. But it seemed there was nothing I could do about that. Even my silly Netflix choices weren't working for me.

The lockdown ended in Istanbul, but we all wore masks outside. I was fortunate enough to get vaccinated. However, my anxiety level was still through the roof. The loudest voices said the vaccines were not a solution. But I was first in line when they became available.

There seemed to be no change in the world. People were dying. Countries began to close borders and go into quarantine. Flights were on. Then they were off. I could feel myself losing it. I had to take care of some important business in Mexico, so I got on a plane and went to stay with my best friend. My headspace seemed somewhat better after my trip to Mexico, where I settled issues that had played on my mind.

I had some very dark days. I've been through a lot of drama and trauma in my life. But even when I was given 6 months to live in 2008, I never experienced anything like this anxious feeling, this physical reaction that my body was going through this past year. It's hard to share because I don't know how to describe it. But I instinctively understood that this is what anxiety felt like.

Türkiye offers a form of free medical care to its citizens. As a foreigner at my age and stage in life, I pay very little for the medical facilities in Türkiye. Age is respected, so the first people to receive the vaccine were over 60's. I was vaccinated once, then had a booster shot. I'd be vaccinated again by the end of the year and had an additional booster. I'd been exposed twice by people that got the disease, and I'd had four shots. I should be calm and feel safe, right? But, I didn't. I wonder if my anxiety was triggered by the vaccines. If it was, so be it. I'd rather suffer from anxiety than die.

And then my best girlfriend in Istanbul died. I had been with her a couple of days before. I told her she should get vaccinated. But she didn't believe in the medicine. I can picture our last day together. We had coffee and dessert in Taksim, the trendy shopping area not far from me and close to where she lived. She showed me the Catholic Church she went to each day for mass. She also volunteered there when they needed an extra pair of hands. We talked about how we'd met in Sultanahmet when she was a tourist, and I had decided I would stay here. She knew Emre, and I knew some of her friends. She thanked me for making her brave enough to follow her heart and live here in Istanbul.

Celine's Catholic Church in Taksim. Every time I walk by, I think of her.

I rarely have more than one close friend in my life at a time. I'm a loner, and yet I've always worked with people. I enjoy my writing, reading, and quiet time. Celine and I would meet every week or so to catch up. It was normal not to hear from her every day. And then, I got the message online from one of her friends. She was in the hospital with Covid.

Within a couple of days, she was dead.

I mourned Celine in my own way. I spoke only with Celine—heart to heart. When I met her, she had many personal issues in the US and the Philippines, where some of her family remained. But after she made the decision to stay here in Istanbul, she found her happiness. She really came into herself and began to enjoy her life and smile more. When I heard she had died, I did what I always do. I buried my feelings. I couldn't talk to anyone who knew her. I was emotionally closed completely.

I think that was the final straw for my sanity. I'm high risk because of my age, even though I'd had the vaccine. So, my own vulnerability was more emotional than physical. But this was a worldwide pandemic. Is the vaccine working? It would turn out that there would be breakthrough cases—whatever that means. And last night, I received news that my vaccinated daughter-in-law and five-year-old grandson tested positive in Paris. They both seem to be doing okay, though, so that's the most important thing. And recently, my daughter-in-law, plus my son, got the new Covid virus and the flu. It was mild because they were vaccinated. I don't know how they can handle all this pressure.

I bring this up because I've always been transparent about my life. I need to apologize to all of you who have ever had psychological illnesses. I didn't understand. I always assumed that mental/emotional illness could be controlled by mind over matter. I believed that with determination, we could get through anything. I'm strong, I told myself. But this year, not long after I lost my friend from the Philippines, I remember standing in the bathroom with this horrible physical shudder in my body. I can't describe the feeling. Except I said to myself: *So, this is what it feels like physically when you fall apart emotionally.*

Faced with these powerful fears, you realize how much your past life affects your current choices. I used to tell people that I "buried" my disappointments and moved on. I think the worries of the pandemic, plus the overwhelming flow of information from around the world, flamed my fears and created my anxiety. I live alone, and it was never a problem before. But this time, loneliness exacerbated my emotional fears and made me completely self-centered. On top of all that, I'm an empath. I *feel* the pain and sadness in the world.

I realize now that I spent a lifetime repressing the memories of the years with my alcoholic father. I asked my sis recently if she remembers the fighting. But she's five years younger. And by her teenage years, my parents had settled in Ottawa, and Dad had retired from the military. They had purchased their first home. My sis said Dad had stopped drinking. Her memories are very different from mine, much more stable and happier. In any case, we recently chatted about our past. She believes that human nature distorts memories. And there are scientific studies that have proven her theory. She's likely correct. I know that we are four kids in the family, separated by 4-5 years from each other. Her experiences with a retired military father were very different than those of my older brother and me. But I dropped the subject. There would be no point in discussing it now.

Why am I sharing these most private thoughts with you? I guess *I've always been an open book.* How appropriate for an author to be able to use that phrase! It took this past year to understand how all the trauma of my early years has impacted my life. It's not that anyone physically hurt me. It's the constant upheaval. And the walls I built around my heart to deal with feeling somewhat lost every time I had to start my life over in a new place. I began to realize that I didn't feel like I belonged anywhere. It's the first time I've acknowledged this even to myself. And maybe that's why I live this way in the present. This anxiety might have nothing to do with the pandemic and everything to do with this recent revelation.

From your comments and the notes I've received, I find that it's helpful to share what I'm going through. It's so vital for you to know you are not alone. It doesn't matter what's happening in our lives; someone else is experiencing similar things. We need to acknowledge our challenges to begin to heal and be whole again.

19

GARBAGE IN GARBAGE OUT

I've concluded that you are never too old to learn new tricks. This past year has also taught me that discipline and routine in my personal life are paramount for my mental and emotional health.

Who likes to read the news? I do. I'm drawn to it first thing in the morning. At least it's in the morning and not late at night. With the time change between Istanbul and the West, the news is rather old, so if Trump is stirring up trouble or there is insurrection at the Capitol Building, I might only learn about it the next day. That's a good thing. I don't allow myself to look at the news past four or five in the afternoon. I find it too upsetting.

Let's take today. for example.

Headlines right now (4 pm. Istanbul) CNN International.

"Spread of <u>misinformation</u>, <u>human trafficking</u>, inciting <u>international violence</u> and more…Facebook leaked documents."

"Biden's refusal of executive privilege claim ignites new firestorm with Trump."

"Rust crew members reportedly used guns with live ammunition before deadly shooting on set."

"CDC moves large European country to its highest level of Covid-19 travel risk."

"Ex-Saudi official: Crown Prince' psychopath' who boasted he could kill sitting monarch."

"Trump allies' 'command center' was a war room for an attempted coup."

I'm asking for an anxiety attack if I take it all in. Nothing has changed in the world. Bad news, sensationalism sells. It takes self-discipline to look away from these disturbing events.

There's considerable controversy over the effect Instagram has on female teenagers. But it doesn't even have to be teenagers. We live in a society that is constantly comparing ourselves to others. There will always be people who have more. This is nothing new. But we are bombarded by negative news daily. And through Instagram and FB, we subliminally compare another's lavish or glamourous lifestyle to our own. Studies show tremendous damage to teenagers, particularly girls, due to their comparisons between themselves and others on these social media platforms.

Do you remember when we would see an accident up ahead on the highway, and all traffic slowed down to look? That's what Instagram, FB, and news sites online have done for today's generation. Multiply the information a hundred-fold and imagine how our psyches are being bombarded without us realizing the damage it is doing to our minds. It's not only that we compare our lifestyles to those of others, but we are also drawn to disasters, accidents, and now wars.

It's a 24/7 assault of news, lifestyle comparisons, and reminders that we are not enough.

When I moved to Mexico in the early 2000s, I did not purchase a TV. There wasn't anything I felt the need to watch as far as I was concerned. I've always hated commercials—the interruptions made me crazy. I would go to the theater if I wanted to see a movie. And I read all the time. If a book turned out to be anything less than I expected or went in a direction that bothered my psyche, I deleted it from my iPad. At one point, I read three books a week. I could download eBooks and take my favorite pastime with me anywhere I went. Then when I got my first MacBook Air, I discovered Netflix and now Prime. I watch the shows I want without being assaulted by negative thoughts or non-sensical commercials. That's how I attempt to manage my mind. I haven't watched TV since flat screens were designed. I don't even know how to turn on a flat screen, and I don't miss it.

Think about this. Do you remember when our parents stayed up to watch the 11 pm News? Now it's 24/7 news on our TV, computer, and phone. It's hard not to watch a 24-hour train wreck. We can't seem to look away. However, if you have books on your iPad, you can decide what to watch and/or read. You control the amount of "news" or commercials you watch.

If we constantly allow all this negative, violent, hopeless, sad news into our minds, we are genuinely screwing with our psyches. How can that be a good thing? There was only one problem with my narrative. During the pandemic so far, it's been really challenging to read a book. Instead, the pandemic news is impossible to look away from, like a car wreck.

So, what did I expect would happen? If I allow my mind to go in that direction...garbage in. Garbage out.

20

THE SOUND OF CHAOS

If you know any of the recent history of Istanbul, there was a coup attempt by the military in 2016. I only read about this after I arrived here. I'm downplaying the issue because I don't know all the details. Hundreds of thousands were involved in this coup attempt.

Since then, thousands of people, anti-Erdogan activists, have been jailed. So naturally, it's still fresh in the minds of the government of Türkiye, and every day it seems someone else is being arrested for ties to the hundreds of thousands that were involved.

The Bridge of Martyrs. I took this photo in the
park across from my apartment.

There was a lot of fallout from this attempt. Thousands were arrested, but assets from those connected to the coup were also appropriated. I've been told that my neighboring office block was seized from one of those criminals who financed the attempted takeover. Apparently, the owner is Iranian, and he's currently in jail.

One day I came out of my apartment, and I heard and saw all this metal being cut, pulled, and thrown to the ground from six stories above. I watched young men come along with human-sized canvas sacks and fill their contrivances with the metal. When the carts were loaded with scrap, the workers used handles over their shoulders to drag the metal away. Their fully loaded contraptions must have been cumbersome. But they came back every hour to take more. After the product was weighed, whoever was in charge got paid for the recycled metal. This went on all day until midnight for months.

The neighbors were suitably outraged. They called the police. Still, the work on the six-story building continued. I spoke with a newly renovated boutique hotel owner on my lane. He was devastated. Who would want to stay on a property fronted by an office complex that looked like a bomb had exploded in the middle of it? A couple called in television camera crews who photographed what was happening and put the story on the news. The reporter wanted to film me when he found out where I lived. I politely refused. I'm aware that journalist have a tough job in the Middle East, and I'm a writer, two reasons I'm smart enough to refuse to be photographed, interviewed, or filmed.

For several months, a couple of dozen men worked all day until midnight—without lights—ripping out all the metal in a six-story, one-block, empty office complex. To watch a building being gutted, the ceilings destroyed, and windows smashed to free the scrap metal is a jarring experience.

It continues to look like a bomb went off but no one is clearing the debris. I feel like I'm living next to a war zone. There is nothing left but an outer shell of a building plus walls, floors, and some roofs. Debris, broken drywall, insulation, and shattered glass are piled high in chunks on each floor. It's incredibly unsettling. And if I think back on it, that's when my anxiety went into overdrive.

This past two weeks, a city truck and workers have started to use red industrial bricks to seal off the lower two levels of the gutted building. I think the purpose is to keep out the homeless, but at this point, none of this makes any sense. There are many layers to something as strange as this, yet it might not be unusual in this city. It could conceivably take that long for issues from the coup attempt in 2016 to go through the courts. And maybe the demolition is court approved. I won't even voice my own thoughts. Foreigners, not unlike little children, should be seen but not heard.

There is no doubt that this event contributed to my mental distress. My creative imagination took over to my psychological detriment. I imagined workers watching me on my little balcony. I feared someone would find a way up on my patio and break into my loft at night. I know it was stupid. These men were doing this job for one purpose only, money. More than likely, they are refugees. They may even be in the country illegally. They wouldn't want to draw undue attention to themselves either. But I hadn't figured any of that out yet. So, paranoia took up space in my mind and would begin to take over my already Covid-anxious psyche. I've lived alone for over twenty years, and I'm good with it. But at times like this, I could have used a 'protector' to reassure me that everything would be alright.

There's never a dull moment in this magnificent city that never sleeps. The smoke and mirrors make it impossible to get to the bottom of what went on. Maybe it's the author in me who sees

mystery everywhere. But in this case, everyone is talking, but no one has the answers. And although I'm curious, I'm also smart enough to know it's not wise to make any guesses or question the wrong people.

After several months, all activity inside the building ceased. A war zone remains on each level of the six-story building. All has been quiet for some time. A small metal office now sits at the front of the lot on the main street. It's staffed by two security guards. And it would be impossible to get inside the building as the lower thirty feet are bricked up. Last night it snowed, and today it looked quite pretty. Now, if my vivid imagination would allow my creative mind to take charge I could get on with my writing, I might even get control over my anxiety.

21

FACE THE FEAR

Somewhere along this journey we call life, we decide that it's embarrassing and shows weakness to discuss our psychological problems. There's a stigma attached to talking about a chemical imbalance and emotional illness. If I hadn't been given a death sentence in 2008 for my physical heart, I might never have learned all the different ways to handle stress and work on my emotional health.

There are things I've never shared with anyone and have only speculated about with my sister. I've asked myself why my early years are blank. I don't really have any memories before the age of eight. I have a weird feeling about that time, and I can't say it's good or bad. Fragments come through occasionally. But it has something to do with a long-passed uncle. I suppose I could go to a therapist and dig it all up. But don't you think some things are best left buried? And with that kind of thinking, problems begin. I've contradicted my last statement about the mind/body connection. But at this age in my life, there is absolutely no one around who would remember that time in my childhood. And what can I do about it now, seventy years later?

I've tried psychiatrists twice. I can't say it has worked for me. I think I misunderstand the process. A psychiatrist is a medical professional who can diagnose and prescribe. I probably need a psychologist or a therapist. I suppose I'm too impatient to work through the junk I've held onto throughout my life. And trying to do so in a country where English is not their first language makes it almost impossible. Notice my excuses are nicely laid out. Procrastination. A friend gave me a name of a female therapist who speaks English. I should call her. But it's unlikely that I will. I know she will want to know my plans, thoughts about the future, etc. She will most likely identify these issues as the cause of my anxiety. But about those plans, these are questions I can't answer. I can't even recall what triggered the events that sent me spiraling downwards. But if I'm candid with myself, both the worldwide pandemic and thoughts about my future caught up with me. And for several months, I lost my ability to write a single sentence. And writing it out has always been my go-to place to handle my emotional world.

So how did I finally deal with the things that cause anxiety in my life? First, I knew I needed to identify the reasons I was anxious. What is holding me back and causing unwanted stress? At least I now know the physical result was panic attacks and anxiety. When I do the inevitable Google search for anxiety, I'm very fortunate that I do not have most of the symptoms. The slight paranoia and fear of the future will work itself out. I know I'm strong. I'm a fighter. I'm used to dealing with everything that life throws at me. Baby Boomers "had it all," and we've fine-tuned our stress into an art form. At one point in our lives, we will pay for all the choices we've had the free will to make. The significant difference in our relationship field is we are not our parents. If we've chosen to have a career, we no longer must "stay in a bad marriage for the children's sake." We can support ourselves financially. And our partners—the ones we were supposed to grow old with—have moved on, also. Martyrdom went out the window with our mothers' generation. For us, Baby Boomers, and Gen X, personal gratification will come first. Even the pandemic didn't completely disturb my psyche. Or at least, that's what I thought.

I have friends in Istanbul that I can call on to help if I need them. I've found the healthcare system to be good anytime I've used it. If I was concerned about my future, I pushed it deep inside and let the worldwide concerns of a pandemic take up time in my mind. Plus, at the beginning of the pandemic, I was in the final edits of my second memoir, Café Confidential. I relived that fantastic time when I sold everything in Mexico to travel to exotic destinations. And I shared how Istanbul became my current home. I didn't really have time to dwell on my future. I was too busy writing and living in my *now*.

I've always been proud of my age. I feel the same today as I did thirty years ago. Sure, I've added a few "Baklava" pounds. But even the Istanbul heart doctor said he could tell I take good care of myself. Over the years, I was never an athlete. I watched my food, rarely over-indulged, couldn't care less if I had a glass of wine, and never smoked nor did drugs. And having younger boyfriends might also be a reason to stay in top form emotionally and physically. But I looked after my health for myself.

And then I had this fateful online chat with my son. It began easy enough but morphed into "what are you doing with your life? At some point, you need to settle down. Where will you go? What will you do? Maybe you can stay with your sister. You are getting old, you know."

I've never been that person that had my life planned out. But this conversation with my son seemed to be the last straw in my mental equilibrium. I know it was said out of concern for me, but he had no idea how it freaked me out. I wasn't aware of how much it disturbed me until it began to sink in. *I have absolutely no plan.* I began to worry. What will I do? Where will I live? If I need care, who will take care of me? If I get ill, how can I be sick in a country where I don't speak the language? I trust the system, but how can I tell someone what is wrong if I'm in distress or have an emergency? In other words, that lovely conversation with my son screwed up my head completely. I'd managed to take a solo dream trip to multiple countries, make it through a worldwide pandemic, self-imposed isolation, months of 'what ifs?' and then that one conversation threw my heart and head into a tailspin. I can't remember if my panic attacks began before this conversation or shortly after. Either way, the timing was terrible.

I looked at various options for my future. I threw out a few feelers to close family and was shut down entirely or ignored. That hurt. But it wouldn't be the first or last time I'd been disappointed in my lifetime. There were many issues I needed to settle, healthcare, and joint bank accounts so others could make decisions for me. As I write this, I remember that I already looked after the banks years ago when I added my older son's name to my most important accounts. I even sent an email to him with an explanation of all this. It was the living arrangements and health care that I had not thought through. I never planned on my life in the Middle East! Wait, let me rephrase that. I never planned on getting old!

While I consider a plan, I need to take control of my mental health around the anxiety these thoughts have created. I've been seriously ill before and come through it because I had a lot of self-belief, faith, and a determination that it was not my time to die. I completely ignored the subject of what would happen if I become incapacitated.

During the early days of the pandemic, I was doing great. I continued to write, enjoyed the quiet of less traffic, and all this gave me time to think and organize my thoughts. Then the deconstruction, the pandemic, and my sons words crept up on my mental health. I stopped writing and I couldn't even read.

I thought I was good. Until I wasn't.

When people I knew began to die, I think my subconscious questioned many of my recent decisions. As wonderful as I find the health care system here in Türkiye, would there be anyone who could translate from English in an emergency? I still don't speak the language; inexcusable, I know. But then I never planned to stay here. Don't even ask me to talk about healthcare which is basically free here and in Canada. But you must be a permanent resident to have all that organized. There is a notary in the office beside my apartment building. I should at least look after a few things while I'm living in this country. But these physical issues can be managed. It was my mind that blindsided me and left me completely freaked out.

I've been through a health scare that left me breathless—literally. To be told I had *six months to live in 2008* and to get my affairs in order is no minor scare. But somehow, maybe because I was younger and braver, I got through it. But this loss of my equilibrium caught me entirely off guard. I was unprepared for anxiety attacks. I had never read about them. I didn't know what was happening to me and couldn't explain the sick feeling in my mind and body.

On top of that, I live alone. I didn't know what I would do if I needed help. I didn't know if my emotional health was related to my physical heart. Maybe I was endangering my life with all this worry. I truly felt that I was in the wrong place at the wrong time for the first time in my life. And in this case, two negatives did not make a positive.

The next step was, what do I do? Where do I go? Where do I belong? Do I want to be alone? If you've been following my story, one thing has been left out of this crisis: Yunus Emre. Yes, he's been an essential person in my life. He's the reason I returned to Istanbul. But he's young. He will never be the husband who will be with me until the end of my life. He's the beautiful, sweet guy who will eventually marry a young woman, have a family, and live a good Muslim life. His life and destiny were pre-ordained by his culture. I've always known this and want these things for him. We've had this discussion out loud. I've brought it up because I know how much he loves children.

Once I realized that I was having emotional health issues, I had no idea what to do. As Brené Brown would say, I felt *vulnerable*, a totally foreign feeling for me. Was all this the result of refusing to live a 'normal life'? One of the things about this culture that I love is the respect I feel older people receive from the community. If I have something wrong, I can walk into my neighborhood pharmacy, describe my symptom, and receive medication. I researched this online, and the way the healthcare system is set up in Türkiye, pharmacists can prescribe most medications. Also, medicine is cheap by North American standards. At the beginning of the year, the government determines the retail price of meds. A lot of this has to do with the fact that there is universal healthcare. Which means that because the government pays for healthcare, they also want to control the costs. There are private hospitals too. I have no idea how the prices compare except they are expensive.

So off I went to my neighborhood pharmacist, who speaks English, and I explained how I was feeling. If you know anything about nervousness/anxiety, the standard medication is SSRIs. She prescribed a low dose of what I later learned was Zoloft. It seemed to help, but after a month, I knew something more was going on with me. I was still getting that sick feeling in the pit of my stomach. And at night, my dreams were far too intense. I began my research and found a university hospital that said they would provide interpreters if the doctor didn't speak my language. I made an appointment.

I know nothing about mental health. I admit I always felt that emotional problems are about 'strength.' I'm strong. I can handle anything that life throws at me, right? I've been divorced and ran away in the middle of the night from a bad marriage. I lost my business with all my assets. I've been raped—more than once. Why would a global pandemic be the thing that brings me down? Or was it simply that I became aware of all the things that *could* happen that *might* leave me alone and helpless for the first time in my life. As I share this with you, I realize that this is the first time I'm acknowledging my own vulnerability. Brené Brown, it might be time for me to read all your books again.

The psychiatrist was mature, pleasant, and spoke some English. I think he understood a lot more than he spoke, or the interpreter allowed him to think about what I was saying while she translated my words. In any case, after half an hour, he sent me on my way with prescriptions. His diagnosis: I was experiencing Panic/Anxiety Attacks!

Usually, I'd go home, do my research, and decide how I was going to move forward. But this time, I went to the pharmacist, got my medicines, and went online to see what he gave me. When I discovered he wanted me to take Xanax, my body went straight into resistance mode even though it was almost the lowest dose possible. Did I mention that addiction ran in my family? There was no way I would take the most addictive drug on the planet. *No way*—I said to myself as I swallowed my first pill.

I realize now that he never explained to me what we were doing and why. The second drug he gave me was an SSRI slightly different than the one the pharmacist had given me when I first began to feel overwhelmed. For four or five days, I did what I was told. But my fear that I would become addicted to a prescription drug overtook my common sense. Dr. Lynda decided she was better and stopped the Xanax. I wanted to throw it out, but I was afraid a stray animal might get into the garbage, eat it, and die! So, I flushed the pills down the toilet.

The attacks would come on at odd times of the day within that month. I could feel the buildup of this strange feeling in my body, and now I recognized it for what it was. I didn't know why I had this panic, but the physical aspects came on quickly and passed after five minutes. During that time, the fear would take over. *Why am I here in Istanbul? What will happen when I get old? Who will I turn to?* This strong, adventurous, sexy woman had turned into someone I no longer recognized. And for the first time in my life, I began to second-guess all these beautiful adventures I'd had, and the experiences and people I'd met. What was I thinking?

I have been blessed with some exceptional people in my life. And when I needed them most, they were there for me. I realized I didn't have to go through this totally alone. And by accident—even though I don't believe in accidents—the right people began to show up and advise me about my health and future.

The most significant was my nephew, the scientist/doctor who lectured me most vigorously about the mishandling of my medication. The words that sealed the deal for me were when he wrote, "Yes, your father was an alcoholic, but you're not! Take the medications the way the doctor prescribed them. There's a reason he is telling you to take it this way. After a month of Xanax, the SSRIs will take over and make you better."

I listened to him because I love and trust him. I returned to the psychiatrist and asked for a new prescription. Again, it lasted for 5 days before I said, I can't do this. Even though the Xanax was a minimal dose, I would fall asleep mid-morning. Who could function like that? Don't get me wrong, the nap was terrific. But there was no way I could live my life feeling tired all the time.

It was back to the drawing board again. I spoke to another friend I admire immensely. My friend is brilliant and successful and operates on a genius level of intelligence. He explained that at one point in his life, he needed Xanax. I was shocked. He asked about my dosage. I explained that I couldn't keep my eyes open after I took it in the morning. He suggested a different way of taking the drug, splitting the pill, and taking the second half within 2-4 hours. Then continue with the way the doctor had prescribed the drugs.

I listened to him for a few days. By then, I was feeling much better. I read more about anxiety. And because I was affected so much by the Xanax, I decided to cut the daily dose in half. I continued but only took a half dose daily. After 10 days, I felt like myself again. I continued doing the regimen, and I took the SSRI in the evening. I couldn't write or focus before I began medication. I knew I was a mess. I also had challenges with my memory. I had no idea if the two were related. Within two weeks, I knew I was healing. I've had no more panic attacks or sick feelings for a few weeks. And I began to write this memoir.

I'm not sure what the future holds. I don't have an addictive personality—unless sugar counts! If I need to take more Xanax at this lower dose, I will. I don't feel strange or tired anymore. I hope this treatment is all I need, but time will tell. I still have three weeks since I cut the dose to half. But I'm functioning on a totally normal level for the first time in several months.

It turns out I was missing a very critical piece of the puzzle. The Xanax was only meant to be taken for 30 days. The idea that I might repeat it off and on was not how the drug was to be taken. My nephew's words broke through the fog in my mind, *you take the Xanax for a month, then the* selective serotonin reuptake inhibitors *or SSRIs take over and make you better.* When will I learn to talk less and listen more?

It was time for Dr. Lynda to retire from playing doctor. The only problem with all of this seems to be that the process is not working for me. It's over six months. I always believed vulnerability was not in my DNA. I was wrong.

22

THIS, TOO, SHALL PASS.

The mornings are the hardest for me. Once I wake up, I must release the night. My dreams have been very vivid for several months now. The good news is I can't always remember them, and I don't try. During the worst of the last several months, I found myself looking for comfort in the routines and habits that had worked for me when I was working through healing my physical heart from a "6 months to live" diagnosis in 2008.

I'm often asked, "What are the secrets of remaining youthful into my 70s?" I think it's both physical and emotional. I've never been a gym rat. I always disliked exercise for the sake of exercising. I try to keep my weight in check. But my Starbucks habit has gotten out of control since the lockdown was lifted. I attempted to buy new jeans the other day and was disgusted with myself. Stretchy leggings work much better. My diet is good, apart from my love of Starbucks Very Berry muffin!

I find it's important to have gratitude. Even in a fragile emotional state, Daily I remind myself how grateful I am for the ability to live my life the way I want. There's something I've not addressed.

I'm basically retired for the first time in my life. I worked outside the home for more than fifty years. The only time I stopped was due to the emergency births of my boys. I had never done anything like my incredible travel over several months in 2019. I never dreamt I would write on my own schedule as a full-time career. Yes, I could have planned things better. But it never crossed my mind that I wouldn't be working full time until the day I died. Maybe that's a Baby Boomer thing. We refuse to accept that we will ever get old! I could still see myself back at work even though I recently passed a significant birthday milestone. I wish I was multilingual. I would love to sell expensive real estate in Istanbul! The architecture in both the old and new buildings is stunning. And the reasons for purchasing real estate in Türkiye are multi-faceted. The stories my real estate friend tells me are intriguing.

With the various challenges I've had lately, I'm working on taking back control of my life. I wake up, shower, and then full-on into my morning meditation with Deepak Chopra on my patio. I find the fresh air and the glimpse of the Bosphorus help stabilize my mind. I might meditate for 10 minutes or keep going up to 30 minutes. Even when the weather is nasty, I still go outside in my winter clothes with an umbrella. I need the grounding to start my day.

After that, I love Adriene's workouts. I will adapt longer or shorter parts of a video. Even fifteen minutes makes a huge difference in how I sit when I'm writing. I focus on the lower back, spine, and posture. I can easily spend an hour on my mind and body before eating breakfast. I never had that kind of exercise consistency when I worked full time. It's not unusual for me to do eight to ten hours in a chair writing, so the morning movement is critical.

Lately, I've been writing, doing research, or watching trashy Real Housewives shows in the evenings. Basically, other than my walks, I live a sedentary lifestyle. Yoga makes me feel stronger. This morning routine centers me, and I can let go of my vivid dreams that have lasted for almost a year.

After the stretches, I make breakfast. The morning is always fruit, yogurt, and muesli. My favorite fruits are bananas, blueberries, and kiwi. But this year, there's a challenge with bananas, something to do with a worldwide virus and shortage that will affect us internationally. It's annoying, but I can work around their ugly appearance if the bananas are not rotting. I mix plain probiotic yogurt with fruit yogurts. And I add in muesli and whatever other fresh fruits I can find at the supermarket. But I do have one very delicious vice I will share with you. Have you ever heard of *Pekmez?* It's grape molasses. And here we mix it with Tahini. Half and half. I add it to my fruit and yogurt. It's my guilty pleasure. It forms a creamy mixture that looks like chocolate sauce, but the two ingredients make it very healthy. I refuse to look at the calorie count!

I no longer drink my white chocolate mocha at Starbucks. I'm trying to cut back and drink only black coffee. It depends on my mood and how long and how much I write. Now summer has arrived, so I often do a few miles of walking if it's not raining. It's beautiful along the waterfront at Galataport. I think the waves calm my soul. Sometimes I will stop and sit in one of the lounge chairs (very modern and fancy, I might add) and fall asleep. Lately I listen to meditations and watch the waves. If I remember, at the end of my day, I will relax and do stretches on the yoga mat while watching baking shows on Netflix, says she, who hasn't had baking powder in her home in twenty years!

I share these things with you because I need to accept that there is more going on with me than "the pandemic screwed up my mind." The change in work focus means I no longer have a boss to kick my butt—even if I was my own boss in the fashion business. I always had other people, obligations and orders to fill. Now it's only me! My discipline can get slack, and the mind can play havoc with my emotions.

I decided to regiment more things in my life. I will share a few of them with you. I recently bought a great herbal tea mix of eucalyptus and ginger and 8 other ingredients from the Spice Bazaar in Istanbul. It's my new favorite hot drink in the evening. I live alone, so mealtimes are up to me. I eat cheese, chicken, turkey, or tuna. If I'm eating at a restaurant, I might have salmon, fish, or lamb. I can't remember the last time I had a steak or beef. I've substituted rice cakes for bread. I could live without meat and may do so at some point. These are the habits I've developed over the past year. With the on/off medication routine, it's been months since I had a glass of wine. It's all good. There's a fantastic bakery I walk by on my way to Starbucks. The pastries are well known. However, I know myself so I have never stepped inside the shop! If I go in once, I'm doomed. My self-discipline will not be able to resist Turkish pastries.

There are so many things in life that we can't control, so I think it's essential to have discipline over the things we can. My happy place is chocolate and sugar. If I ate only pure dark chocolate, it could be a good thing. But I don't, so it's not! There is no junk food in my house mainly because it won't last twenty-four hours! My self-control is limited. There's no one to lecture me about my eating habits. As my younger son used to tell me: "I'm the boss of my life!" So, if it's to be, it's up to me.

Nobody is perfect. Coke Zero is my vice. I drink lots of water all morning and all evening. I'm happy I never smoked. That's a problematic drug to quit. My good skin and freckles keep me looking youthful. Although I admit to the odd nip and tuck twenty years ago while I lived in Mexico.

I mentioned walking. I've never been an athlete. I've cycled, skied, and swam—none of these events were what we could call exercise by anyone's standards. My daily walks are an opportunity for me to photograph and think about my current WIP. After writing for a few hours, I walked the entire seaport area. I had lunch at a small outdoor chicken doner stand and sat in the sun watching the ferries come back and forth from the Asian to the European side of Istanbul. I try to keep moving. I admire all my super active friends. I know I need exercise, or my brain doesn't function, and my memory loss is more significant. It's also part of taking charge of the long-term anxiety I've felt since last winter. All these things help me feel more in control of my life.

Cruise ships arriving at the new Galataport area

The most Instagramable shot in Galataport! I have no idea
how the ice-cream tastes and I refuse to find out!

I follow my morning routine of meditation and exercise. It's no
longer an option but a necessity. I was walking on a bustling street
during the beginning of my dark period when I felt a weird
sensation begin to take over my body. I didn't know it was anxiety
at the time; I simply knew I was in trouble. Istanbul is such a hectic
city. Everyone is always in a rush. No one was looking at me, so
I instinctively turned to Tapping. I haven't used that technique in
twelve years. I would have learned how to do it in 2008 when my
physical heart was broken. I will link to Tapping at the end of the
book. The official name is EFT or Emotional Freedom
Techniques. It's an effective way to reduce anxiety symptoms such
as excessive worry, irritability, sleeping challenges, and difficulty
concentrating.

Definition:

Tapping various points (the energy points and flow channels the Chinese have always referred to as meridians) along your eyebrows, nose, jaw, chin, throat, collarbones, armpits, chest, and belly can be soothing. Tapping these various points in a defined top-to-bottom order and in a continuous cycle several times in a row is said to release anxiety, lower stress, and get you back to feeling more centered.

When I was diagnosed with Idiopathic Dilated Cardiomyopathy in 2007/8 and given 6 months to live, I practiced many things to calm my fears. It amazes me how this technique came into my mind when my body needed it. I didn't think twice. I took three fingers of my right hand and began to tap on the bony Karate-chop area of my left hand. I repeated whatever mantras I could remember and tapped on the various meridian points on my upper body. Three lanes of evening traffic surrounded me as I walked across at the green light, Tapping my forehead. I knew everyone was too busy rushing, listening to the news or music, rather than paying attention to what I was doing. And it worked for me. The episode passed.

It finally dawned on me that if I had the need to resort to Tapping, it meant I had more significant problems. But at the moment, I was grateful I'd learned this technique and began to use it in bed at night. I would accompany my Tapping with mantras developed over the years. I could fall asleep within a few minutes. I recently had a conversation with a friend who asked me if I had tried tapping. I thought it was remarkable that many of these techniques have become mainstream. If we embrace them, we can do a lot for our emotional balance. It would be wonderful if I could develop habits that eliminated the need for medication. But then I tell myself with everything going on in the world, pandemics, wars, and poverty, I am grateful that my only issue is ongoing anxiety.

I turned to many holistic practices that helped me get through a *6-months to live diagnosis in 2008*. I learned how to do Reiki. I still need to refresh myself on the techniques and prayers of Reiki and start a practice to help heal my emotional response to this universal anxiety. Right now, it's a practice I could also do before bed. It might help me with my far-too-vivid dreams. I did some research for Reiki practitioners here in Istanbul but didn't find any. I'm sure they exist. I need to dig a bit deeper.

I've found all the Reiki symbols I would use when doing Reiki on myself. And I've discovered distance Reiki that practitioners are doing on YouTube. I've been listening and absorbing the energy now for the past hour.

I mentioned earlier that I went back to Mexico to care for some unfinished business. While visiting my friend Jeannie, I went for a Traditional Chinese Medicine treatment. I felt more relaxed after. The practitioner provided me with some herbal products. But I must admit I was afraid to take them. Maybe that was a part of my paranoia and anxiety at the time. I left some of the products with my friend. I've always been careful what I put into my body (sugar excepted!). But that's ignorance on my behalf. I did my research when I returned to Türkiye. The three products she gave me were not legal to sell or use in Türkiye! It turned out to be a good thing I'd left two of them behind with my friend. If I'd had my luggage searched at the airport, I could have been refused entry.

There are many practices we only turn to in time of need. But the way we take vitamins as a preventative to deteriorating health, we should also make these alternative practices and products a part of our daily life instead of waiting until we are scrambling for answers. We could call it emotional maintenance.

How did I manage to reach my seventies without falling apart? I didn't. I got halfway through the decade before I learned what it means to be challenged emotionally. In the past I was more than likely too busy trying to keep my head above water to recognize the signs at the time. I've gone to three different doctors, and each have prescribed Xanax once a day for thirty days. I've almost finished my six-week regimen of Xanax and SSRI's.

I truly understand why 'benzos' are so addictive. I also accept that, in my case, medical intervention was necessary. But I think I'm a superwoman, and I will have no problems when my dose is finished. I didn't get 'high' nor feel anything strange while on Xanax. The dosage was also low, and I cut the pills in half and only took them once a day. I simply felt like myself. I have 5 half tablets put away for an emergency. But so far, I don't need them. The SSRIs have taken over. And this morning, by noon, I'd forgotten to take any of my meds. That's a great sign that I'm recovering. I don't think about Xanax at all.

Up until recently, the mornings were the worst. I'd do yoga, eat a healthy breakfast, and keep myself distracted until the meds kicked in. I'm still taking a half dose of a medication my Cardiologist recommended for anxiety the last time I saw him—it's a beta-blocker. I will ease off of it because it was prescribed only for anxiety, not for my heart. But I'm not ready to let it go yet. And again, I don't know if there will be repercussions.

As I write this, I realize how fortunate I have been with my health. Lots of people must be suffering from this Covid nightmare. And so many have died. For those who have recovered or have not yet had the disease, anxiety levels must be very high. If you are one of them, you have my sympathies. I am counting my blessings as I share my story with you.

Here's how I am dealing with my new healthier normal.

A typical day starts with releasing dreams that are not bad but are particularly vivid. My dream world often carries the characters from my Netflix shows, so I don't allow anything dark, dangerous, or mysterious to enter my psyche in the evening before bed. Food shows and light romantic comedies are great. Real Estate and design shows are relaxing too. I've watched Emily in Paris several times. Even the bitchy housewives series are a fun distraction for me. I'm really enjoying the East Indian Netflix shows. Some of the Indian shows are a bit difficult to understand because the Indian English accent is so thick. I realized one morning that all the characters in my dream the night before were speaking with an East Indian accent! I loved Decoupled. It's a story of a modern Indian couple in Mumbai who decide they must divorce. The writing is excellent. The show had me giggling all night. And of course, that couple was in my dreams—accent and all!

I practice what I preach. This morning I was feeling off from my dreams, so I needed extra help. I did a Deepak Chopra meditation for focused on healing, after my yoga. To shake off the night, I need to get out of the house right away. It's December, so it is chilly and rainy today, so I took my umbrella and walked the waterfront anyway. And then found a spot to sit and do my Tapping technique. I'm so grateful for all these habits I picked up at various times in my life. As I tick off the boxes on my "should-do" list each day, I know I'm progressing in my mental state.

Are you wondering why I'm sharing all this with you? If you're not, I am. The one word that I repeatedly hear about my answers on Quora and my first two memoirs, LOVE The Beat Goes On, and Café Confidential is *inspiring*. I know that what I'm going through is familiar to many. Even though our lives can look perfect to an outsider, we never really know what's happening inside another's body, mind, and soul. I hope my words reassure you that you are not alone on this journey we call life. And maybe something I write will resonate with you so you can dig into some of my healing methods or get professional help. You might also share my thoughts with a friend who needs them.

23

SEX: "IT IS HORRENDOUS, BUT THEN IT'S MAGNIFICENT."

L et's talk about sex. Did I make you smile? Men, you can skip this chapter unless you to better understand the women you love. Then, I invite you to read on!

Women are particularly neglectful about health issues. We are usually so busy looking out for everyone else we forget about ourselves. It takes a good girlfriend to advise us when we are on the wrong track. Outsiders can see what is happening when we can't.

Our physical health and enjoyment are certainly as important as our emotions. I did some research about sex as we age. A poll conducted by the AARP found that sexual desire runs deep among people in their 50s, 60s, 70s, and beyond. When we meet a potential mate at any stage of life, we will not connect unless there is "attraction." That initial response to a man or woman is sexual, a physical connection, a need for intimacy. This feeling does not go away as we age. But it may change form in terms of our physical abilities and challenges. There are lots of good articles on the internet to give you up to the date information.

I have spoken with other women about their sexuality later in life. I'm not a medical doctor nor a therapist, so it's not my intention to advise you whether to continue to have sex into your 60s and 70s. Many couples are in second or even third marriages. Divorce or illness often determines how sexually active mature women or men will be in the second half of their lives. The loss of a beloved partner can change your attitude towards future intimacy and sexual desire. These are personal issues that most likely need to be discussed between couples.

I read a great article about a **sex study on heterosexual women up to 94!** Right? Who would have thought that elderly women would be included in research on sex! I know what you're thinking! "Lynda will be that 94-year-old woman!" You're probably right!

The study was published in July 2017 by researchers from Indiana University in partnership with OMGYes, an online interactive learning tool that teaches users about female pleasure. Researchers conducted their national online survey in 2015, and included 1,055 primarily heterosexual women (91 percent) between 18 and 94 years of age. More than half of the respondents were married, and 65 percent identified as white. And they are having much more sex than you can imagine! AARP found in their surveys that sex can help strengthen intimate relationships at any age while it eases stress and boosts overall health. For seniors, sex can also restore a feeling of vitality, says Erica Goodstone, Ph.D., a certified sex therapist and licensed mental health counselor who works with many older couples and singles. "It's part of being truly alive."

It's up to you and your partner to determine what works for each other. I acknowledge that men have their own physical aging issues regarding sex. This is a conversation that we must have with our lovers. As a Baby Boomer I'm from the 'free-love' generation in the '60s. Still, I'm shy to talk about sex with a partner. I was brought up Catholic. Sex outside marriage was a sin. Inside marriage, sex was reserved for procreation. Sex was never discussed when I was growing up. We just knew that it was an immoral activity outside marriage that felt so good. I look back now, and I can say, "wow!" I hope the teachings have changed since my day in Catholic private schools.

I paused writing to read an article recently published on Huffington Post. You all know about my addiction to Netflix. I re-watched many old movies and some contemporary classics like **Sex in the City**. When it came out, we watched it for the fashion, but it also reflected the mores of the time. There's a controversy brewing over the lack of sex talk in the sequel, **Just Like That**. The author Melinda Buckley of the following Huff Post quote went to see the Off-Broadway show by Candice Bushnell, **Is There Still Sex in the City**. Age seemed to have tamed down the conversation. The reviewer had this to say about the issue of sex in our 50s, 60s, and beyond.

I couldn't agree more with this exchange from Season 2 of "Fleabag" When 33-year-old Phoebe Waller-Bridge says she's heard menopause is horrendous, 58-year-old Kristin Scott Thomas quips back, "It is horrendous, but then it's magnificent."

"It is magnificent to be released from that hormonal pull. I feel freer than ever since I've stopped chasing estrogen. I'm finally becoming who I'm meant to be. I'm also happily remarried. I met

my now-husband when I was 62, and we absolutely have chemistry, but we also have so much more." Added Kristin.

Candace Bushnell might not be willing to talk about sex after 50, and we'll have to see if "And Just Like That" ever broaches the topic. In the meantime, I'll start. We need to talk about sex, we need to share our stories, and then we need to see those stories reflected back to us. Because we are beautiful and vital and sexy, waaay past the expiration dates imposed on us by pop culture.

And to you lovelies stepping up to the edge, I say that sex after 50 (and beyond) can be fabulous! Don't let anyone tell you otherwise.

Written in Huff Post by Melinda Buckley

Even though I'm in a relationship, if I want a different one, I can think of two people who are gladly waiting in the wings for me to acknowledge their attention. Both men are between the ages of 35-40. It's hard for me to tell. If I ask, I would be showing an interest on a personal level that I have no desire to pursue. I don't like to play with someone's emotions.

The other day I took a taxi to get photos for my government permits. The taxi driver was cute, sexy, and conniving. He was probably in his early 30s, and he asked for 8 times the money of what the trip was worth! He was using a legal taxi, but the meter was off. We agreed on 4x ($7.00 USF) because I knew it would be a fun conversation. And then he hit on me. He kept watching me in the mirror and smiling. Finally, he said, "How old are you? 40, 45, or maybe 49?" That compliment alone was worth the overpriced cab ride! I just laughed and enjoyed the harmless banter.

Fifteen minutes later we got to our destination, and he was still working on me. He passed his phone and asked me to put my number in it. I'm totally used aggressive Turkish men. Generally, guys are slower to move in for the kill. But he knew time was not on his side. As we say in sales, *if you don't ask for the business, for sure, you will not get it!* He thought he had a 50/50 chance of closing the deal. All I wish to say is if you are open-minded and want to be in a relationship even though you are older, it's out there, waiting for you! The secret is to be open, smile, and not be afraid of rejection. And, no, I did not give him my number.

There are enough terrible things in the world. At least, I hope my random thoughts can be part of the solution instead of part of the problem. This sleek, sexy operating machine might not be what it was thirty or forty years ago. But I believe I can be judged by the size of my heart and the laughter in my eyes rather than my less than taut Suzanne Somers butt. Although apparently, I still have a hot butt!

I've been in relationships with younger men for most of my life. I would say I qualify as an authority. And believe me when I say I never pursue. However, if the men are decades younger, which has been my case, a warning must come with the decision to proceed. Someone's heart will be broken. A life-long relationship with a much younger man will come with an expiry date. But then, I may have a slightly distorted opinion. Theere are no guarantees in life and love at any age. Love is a risk. We need to decide if it's worth the risk to open our hearts.

At any age in life, stay in shape. Find a physical activity that you like to do. I walk and try to do yoga every day. Yes, menopause will be a 'pause' while your body goes through material changes.

But once it's over, your sleek, sexy operating machine no longer has mood swings nor the physical discomfort that monthly periods bring. You will experience a whole new level of freedom. And for the first time since you were fifteen, you no longer base each day's decision on emotions. I'm not saying our choices to enter a relationship will always be right, nor will the relationships be long-lasting. But we can finally look past our biology-centered emotions and live our lives heart-centered. Now I've said all this, assuming that a relationship or partnership is crucial to you. Maybe it's not important at all.

Is this what it means to be a wise woman? Many of you might not approve of or even understand my life. Or my relationship with younger men. Sometimes, I don't understand myself. But it's interesting that I've never experienced a dirty look from someone in this Muslim country or felt like my lifestyle and friendship with a young man was wrong or unacceptable. However, in the interests of full disclosure, it's never been put to the Muslim family test. And it never will. I would absolutely be an unacceptable partner for my young man. Our parents' generation had their own mores and challenges. And it will be different with our children and their children. All we can do is live our best life. I want to be authentic. I will continue to follow my heart in all things.

And please, look after your physical body. Women need to go to a gynecologist. And men, go get yourself checked out too! Even though you might not be engaging in a relationship, take care of yourself. You don't want any serious problems because you neglected to have your yearly checkups.

And by the way, in the interests of self-care, there's nothing like a good orgasm to help you relax and fall asleep at night, alone or with a partner! I feel the daily female orgasm deserves its own chapter. If self-pleasure has not been a part of your sexual practice, it's never too late to start.

24

HEALTHY LIFESTYLE

What constitutes a healthy lifestyle for you? I'm often asked what is my secret. I look and much younger than my years. I usually smile and accept the compliment. But the question deserves an answer, so I will share some thoughts with you.

I've never been an athlete of any kind. I do more now than I ever did. But if your exercise consists of walking the Galataport waterfront, you need to add other things to your day to make up for your laid-back routine.

I love the contrast between the new Galataport cruise ship terminal
and the existing older section of shops, cafés, and culture.

When I was younger, I had good and bad lifestyle examples. I can remember an overflowing ashtray sitting on the arm of dad's Lazy Boy chair. Eventually, he gave up smoking. The ashtrays disappeared. But if you stood outside his closed workroom door, you might catch the odd whiff of cigarette smoke. I never smoked, and I can't remember the last time I had a drink of alcohol. I've never understood smoking. It's responsible for additional facial lines, weak lungs, and an aging body. Then you will need plastic surgery to get rid of those facial lines, which can become expensive. It's never too late to stop bad habits. Cutting back is better than nothing. Smoking comes with a cancer warning on the package for a reason. Give it up! Your body and mind will thank you. In the meantime, you would think the Turks invented cigarettes. They smoke, especially the young ones. But they will learn. Hopefully, before it's too late.

I'm not against alcohol in moderation. I've been on anxiety meds, so I would not take a chance of having a bad reaction. Still, it's probably a year since I had a glass of wine. I've never had hard alcohol, but I like a glass of rosé or dry white wine. If I never drank alcohol again, I wouldn't miss it. Maybe it stems from my dad being an alcoholic during my teenage years. I don't have memories of words of wisdom from my dad. But that's life. My father eventually stopped drinking, too late to make a difference to my bad memories. Yes, I moved on from the negative experiences. I'm grateful for the lessons I learned about addiction very early in life.

A healthy body.

My mom was born on a farm in Ontario, Canada. When you lived on a farm almost one hundred years ago, you ate whatever you could grow. Fresh farm-to-table was the way it was done. So a healthy family was the norm for us. If my mother was alive today, she would have turned one hundred years old this past year! Where did the time go, and why is it moving so quickly?

We grew up with balanced meals and no junk food in our house. But I do remember canned veggies. Peas particularly! I hated them and still do! We didn't have the international winter food distribution that's available today.

Mom was a great baker. I've never been able to replace her date squares or ginger snap cookies! Today we're more fortunate. It doesn't matter where you are in the winter; you can get fresh fruit and vegetables flown in from all parts of the world. We have no excuse for not eating well. My mother's example of good food and simple cooking taught me how to look after myself as I got older. And maybe that's why I've been relatively healthy—if you don't count my "6 months to live" diagnosis in 2008. But that was from a "swollen heart." I carried a lot of sadness in my heart and earned that diagnosis on a metaphysical level. I will always believe in the mind/body connection to our health.

Covid-19 certainly put a damper on the last two years. Due to lockdowns, exercise consisted of anything you could do in your home. Fresh produce was limited to whatever the tiny local grocery stores received. I could see the shortages. But now, as we move out of quarantines and lockdowns, shopping for food is better. Food is the most essential aspect of Turkish life apart from the mosque. I know I've been eating much healthier since I came to this country in 2019. I shop for fresh food daily. I'm trying foods I've never eaten before. I've got a steady diet of tuna, turkey, chicken, veggies, and lots of fruit and yogurt. I've moved on from my weakness for Starbucks white chocolate mocha. I'm drinking more black coffee in my mission to drop my "Covid" weight. And I do have the occasional Very Berry muffin. I'm trying to cut back on sweets, but not every day is a win! And for optimal health, don't forget about water. Water makes everything better. I like mine cold. I keep a plastic bottle in the freezer because I like a layer of ice about a third of the way up the bottle then I add more water. When I work or read, I'm always drinking water. My guilty pleasure is Coke Zero and chocolate. And maybe, the Caramel Waffle Starbucks cookie! No one is perfect!

Food is essential, but so is exercise.

I'm a writer. I sit on my cute butt all day long. Yes, I've tried the walking desk and the exercise bike desk. I'm a woman, and I should be able to multi-task, but I can't seem to get these multi-purpose desks to work for me. If I was more diligent about my writing, I would have to make a change. But my daily yoga practice has incorporated lots of neck, back, arm, and leg stretches to keep my body in shape. I try to walk for at least an hour or more every day, in good or bad weather. One thing I was lucky to have in Mexico and here, I can write outside. I was often oceanfront, working under a palapa on the beach in Mexico. In Istanbul, I no longer have a boss. I can write on my own patio and outside at my Starbucks office. I can sit under the heat lamps in winter, which is cozy. And I'm surrounded by the odd digital nomad and many Turks who like their cellphone and cigarettes. If you can call city air fresh, I'm getting plenty of 'fresh' air. Some days I long for my Covid-19 mask.

It's the beginning of January. The temperature is in the '50s. Yes, I still think in Fahrenheit. I'm on a busy street in a city of seventeen million people. I'm also oceanfront, so that helps a bit with the pollution. I have no problem tuning out everything going on around me. My son tells me it's called 'white noise.' It's easy to focus on my current project. Two great benefits of the mask are warmth in the mild yet chilly winters in Istanbul, and it's a partial barrier to cigarette smoke and car emissions. Even though it's 4:30 pm and rush hour has arrived, my entire area is still in the Green on the air quality index.

It doesn't matter if you are currently inactive; habits can be changed. It's never too late to make better choices. My daily yoga practice only began a few years ago—after my 2008 '6 months to live' diagnosis. Some mornings I do 20 minutes, other's 35. But if I skip the morning, I do it in the evening.

Now If I could only learn the Turkish language, I would really be impressed with myself!

25

SEXY IS WHAT SEXY DOES.

The trick to *being* sexy is *feeling* sexy.

I have been obsessed with my weight my entire life. I always thought I was overweight. Maybe I was when I was younger. But sometimes, our view of ourselves starts at puberty, and we never believe we are anything but this rather flat-chested square-looking eleven-year-old.

This photograph of myself comes to mind. I think I was maybe 9 years old here. I'm guessing because my sis is five years younger. My brother was in the Army cadets, and I think he might have been going off to summer camp. You can see my ballet stance from my feet. I considered myself dumpy, chunky, and flat-chested, and I stayed that way in my mind. But if you look at this picture, I was a pretty girl. We were a good-looking family. But somehow, I never thought that I was attractive. I can't blame it on the media. We didn't have the internet, IG, or FB to bombard us with examples of the perfect body or the perfect hair. I only realized I was attractive when I was older.

In the '50s, my older brother went off to military
Camp, and me with my baby sister

My mother constructed my first bra from a remake of a pale pink
satin bra sent from my Aunt Rita. Hand-me-downs were the
norm in my world at that time. For some reason, we thought Aunt
Rita was rather exotic. She lived in the exciting city of Toronto
while we lived on an army base in military housing in Edmonton,
Alberta. She may have been divorced or single at the time. I
believe she had a career and obviously a little extra money to spend
on herself because her lingerie hand-me-downs were beautiful.

185

Mom would spend hours on her sewing machine to remake Aunt Rita's things. And then Mom would also buy fabric and make our clothes. She taught me how to sew in my early teens so I could make my own clothes. I was a quick learner. I went on to sew a turquoise velvet shift dress and topped it with a white boucle coat for my high school graduation dance. I would use the skills my mother taught me in my professional career years later.

But self-esteem is formed very early in life. When I looked in the mirror, I saw a plain girl with reddish-blond hair, freckles, and no body curves. That image of myself stayed in my mind for many years. It seems like forever.

I watched a Netflix series last night called *What the Love* with Karan Johar. He's an Indian filmmaker and heartthrob. I recognized him from Bollywood Wives. (Yes, I've spent far too much time on Netflix this year!) In this show he has chosen a dozen people to help them in their quest to find love. The series is set in Mumbai and is a modern approach to matchmaking.

One of the first things he does, is have the contestant sit with a sketch artist. Karan has the woman or man face forward away from the artist and describe his/her own facial features. When the artist is finished, she hands the sketch to the contestant. Then the artist faces the contestant and does her own drawing of what she sees when she is looking at the person. They are always very different. There is an ugliness and insecurity to how we see ourselves. We may have formed our opinions from an unrealistic view of our faults, or from comments made to us by relatives or ex-boyfriends and girlfriends. But there is no question that we re-enforce our negative feelings about what we consider our flaws and unfortunately, we focus on them and often carry them with us our whole lives.

I never thought I was sexy. Not even as a young adult. It was only in my later years, after fifty, that I truly came into my own. Then I understood I had 'something' that guys liked a lot. I still think it's my flirty personality and wit. But men of all ages still find me attractive. I once read that 'youth is wasted on the young.' In my case that was certainly true. But sexy is not only about how we appeal to our preferred sexual partners, but it's how we feel about ourselves. I don't think it's based only on our bodies. It's about acceptance of our true self. It's about finding the good and focusing on those things that make us beautiful. And those things must be more than the physical.

I don't think that sex appeal should determine a woman's worth. But what I do think is confidence, knowing who you are and what you want in life, is sexy. The things that make a person attractive are your inner beauty, compassion, self-love, awareness of the world, and empathy for the challenges we all face. And, that type of beauty comes in all shapes, sizes, colors, and ages. If you believe what I'm writing, then you know that sexy is an inside job. No one can give us self-esteem. And with time we learn that even if we make mistakes by choosing the wrong partners, no one can take it away. It's sad it can take a lifetime for some of us to understand how to love ourselves.

26

OF ALL THE THINGS I'VE LOST,
I MISS MY MIND THE MOST.

I love to watch children play. They don't need a toy to find life entertaining. Anything that catches their innocent eyes is fun. It begins in the crib when we place mobiles across the top. If something is hanging, those little eyes are fascinated. Eventually, a hand or foot reaches up to try to move the hanging toy. Giggles emerge. Delight ensues. And adults watch in wonder.

With each passing year, we lose that childish wonder and allow ourselves to fall into the adult trap. Instead of finding joy in the simple things around us, we focus on our problems. If you have a paper and pen beside you, take a second to write down a list of your problems; then write a list of things that give you joy. I don't even have to ask. It's easier to list the things that trouble you because that's what we focus on every day. Advertisements on our phones, computers, and TVs tell us what we are missing. They insist we need *more things*. And these objects will make our lives perfect. We wonder why we become restless and unhappy.

Beauty and happiness are inside jobs.

Advertising is why I haven't turned on a television in over twenty years. Any news I need will show up on my computer. But even then, I must take care. If I follow a link to what looks like an interesting article, then I'm likely to be assaulted with internet ads. It's like a maze I can't find my way out of, but I eventually do. It's a combination of too much-unwanted stimulation and an infringement on my peace of mind that drives me crazy. If I need something, I will do my research, then buy it. Even that has become a challenge. Whatever you look at on your computer or phone follows you for days. Even if it is something as simple as the weather.

I don't remember exactly when I began to fall apart.

I was fine when I decided that I would self-isolate when the first hints of Covid showed up in the news. I was still able to write. The 'aloneness' was a novelty. But when Emre's father died and then my friend Celine, everything changed for me. That's over two years now. The only thing that saved me was my writing. I was well into writing The Istanbul Heist and Café Confidential. I was okay as long as I had work to do on those books. I don't want to dwell on this darkness that has lasted far too long. I only bring it up because our minds are far more fragile than our bodies, as I've mentioned before. I understand this better than ever now. I would love to say my one month of Xanax was the end of my emotional meltdown, but it turned out not to be the case.

We've lost control of mind junk, *and* we need to find a way to filter what we allow to access our minds and hearts. What I watch on Netflix in the evening makes its way into my dreams. Always. I don't know if it did before our current worldwide disease, but in my case, I'm acutely aware that it does now because of my fragile mental state. But the fact that I can write this memoir is a huge sign that I'm taking back control of my headspace and hopefully healing. This is the fourth time I am re-writing and editing, and it won't be the last. I will ask you in advance to be forgiving of my errors. I do write from my heart and sometimes overshare. But this is me.

I'm acutely aware that I still have my wild dreams. When I choose something on Netflix or Prime, I have to ask, *will this upset me?* I'm now an expert on food from around the world, the art of making pastry and chocolate confections! I want to distract myself, and these series will do that. But, if there is any conflict, bickering, hair pulling, or name-calling, I pass the show immediately. I've spent a lifetime dealing with divorce, loss, and even a 6-months-to-live diagnosis, but my psyche has never been as impressionable as it is right now.

I write all this, so you will know you are not alone.

Whether you are married, living by yourself, divorced, or a student in college, you are more than likely affected emotionally by the collective fear. Lockdown finished, and masks came off but still the after affects linger. You might be surrounded by people like I am on the patio at my Starbucks office, yet I can still feel like I'm alone. But you are not alone—unless you want to be.

We owe it to those who have lost their lives to live for them. I often think of my friend Celine. I might have been the last person who spent time with her before she was hospitalized. She must have gotten very sick quickly because she did not reach out to me. No one else would have known how to reach me except one young Turkish student who had become a close friend of hers. She might have listed him as next of kin. He sent me a message on FB. Due to the fear of infection, no one could go to the hospital. All we could do was pray. Within a few days, she died.

I'd been exposed for sure when I was with her a couple of days before she was hospitalized. But I did not get the virus. At the time, I had been vaccinated once and then boosted. Now I'm vaccinated twice and have had a booster for each vaccine. Do they work? I have no idea. I've not caught the virus, so something works in my favor. I can't think of one person I know who did not get the virus—even a few who were vaccinated. The vaccinated friends and family said their symptoms were milder. Although there is so much skepticism about the efficacy, I can't imagine the level of anxiety I would have if I hadn't been inoculated.

It's two years later. The mask mandate for outside was lifted in Istanbul weeks ago. I feel naked without my mask. There were breakthrough cases. I know of some myself. Some never had the booster. It wasn't available at first. But no matter what anyone says, I'll take the vaccinated odds anytime.

The World Health Organization believes countries do not report a valid number of cases and deaths. Things are moving so quickly that the statisticians can't keep up with the data. I have a fellow author who has a large following on FB. It breaks my heart to see him reporting negatively on the vaccines. It's one thing to have an opinion about politics or something that doesn't cause deaths. But maybe he has never lost anyone close to him. When my boyfriend's family members got sick, the vaccine had not yet been developed. I can see the pain in his eyes two years later when he speaks of his dead father.

There is so much controversial information out there about the vaccines. And we all know how a percentage of our friends love to be anti-anything. But what if the conspiracy theorist is wrong about the vaccine? What if the vaccines do have some protection against the virus? What if, due to his strong disbelief in the vaccine's efficacy, even one of his followers dies? The FB disclaimer notices are useless in a situation like this.

All I know is I am super grateful to be in Türkiye. I was offered the vaccine as soon as it was available in Istanbul. The medical board determined that the elders were the most vulnerable. And even though I have a temporary resident permit and am neither a citizen nor a permanent resident, I was vaccinated before anyone I know. I'm grateful. Did the vaccines affect my mental stability? Who knows for sure? I know that if I didn't take the shot, I would have experienced a dangerous level of anxiety. If the vaccines affected my already fearful mental/emotional stability, it's something I would prefer to handle than a physical illness that could lead to death. And although the signs of a lingering pandemic have faded, I still feel naked when I don't wear my mask.

Could this be our world war?

We know the enemy, but have we really found the right weapon to fight this mutating virus. It's like living in the middle of a science fiction movie. And now that it seems to have passed, what will be next? We all know someone who died during this battle. The pandemic has caused conflict among so many people. It's probably led to more deaths than necessary because of this distrust in any kind of authority.

It took a worldwide pandemic to realize that we are all in this together. No matter what we believe, what we do affects those around us. #WeAreAllOne.

27

LIFE HINGES ON A COUPLE OF SECONDS YOU NEVER SEE COMING.

I met my ex-husband over forty years ago. We were introduced to each other by a mutual friend. I don't remember anything about our first meeting. When I mention this, what goes through my mind is some guy lurking, checking me out from across a room. After getting to know him, I remember thinking about how good-looking he was and what great children we would make together. I'm smiling at the way my mind works. We went on to have two boys and were together for over twenty years.

When I left him and moved to Mexico, we didn't have much more to say to each other. But we do have our adult boys in common. Now, after several years of very little communication, we have re-connected. I think it's a good thing. After all, you can't spend that much time together without some commonality. Are you wondering if we would ever become a couple again? No. Why? I don't want to be in charge again. I can see looking back that I made all the big decisions. Where we would live, what we would do. Should we move out to Western Canada? I no longer have the need nor want the responsibility to be *that person* in a couple again. We can be friends, but I don't want to be the strong one anymore. I also don't want to entrust my happiness to anyone but myself. Each day I say to myself: I love myself. I will get through whatever life throws at me. I am enough. But, yes, we seem to have become friends again.

My last three years in Istanbul have been very different on many levels. First, I've retired from my career in sales to focus on my writing and travel. I love that I was able to do that. But along came the pandemic, and all travel was put on hold.

I don't miss my Mexican life, but there are times when I think fondly of the people. Salespeople are fun to be around. You must have lots of confidence and be very strong emotionally to work with people and handle the constant rejection of a sales career. And my acquaintances shared one thing in common: we all left our lives in Canada, the US, or somewhere else in the world to live and work in Mexico. So, our sense of adventure and self-belief creates a stimulating environment. There are times when I think of that camaraderie. It might have helped me get through this pandemic better than I'm doing alone in Türkiye. But that's what I love about social media. I can keep in touch, check Instagram, comment on FB, and continue to have friendships, both new and old, worldwide.

After liquidating my life in Mexico and beginning the journey of a lifetime, I think this should be my epitaph: *Life hinges on a couple of seconds we never see coming.* Those couple of seconds happened on a fateful chilly morning in early March 2019. I took a few seconds to sit down on an ancient stone ledge in Sultanahmet, Istanbul. I'd arrived late the evening before from

New Delhi, and within the next forty-eight hours, I would be in Jerusalem, Israel. Istanbul was never on my radar. Of course, I'd heard of the city a gazillion years ago when I studied history and the Ottoman empire. But I couldn't place it on a map, and I thought Türkiye was in Europe. You might say I was here, in Istanbul, by accident.

I thought I had myself and my journey figured out. But w*hile man plans, God laughs.* That definitely summed up my meeting with a very young handsome Turk on that chilly morning in March. The older I get, the more I appreciate serendipity. I no longer question long lineups in traffic, canceled flights, or "bumps in the road." Everything happens for a reason, even if we can't see it at the time. That morning changed the direction of my life.

I didn't know the Turkish language but no worries. If you are one of the "boys of Sultanahmet," you speak English. Your job is to entertain the tourists and eventually bring them to your shop so the boss can sell the couple or, in my case, the single woman, a Turkish carpet. I understand the process. I come from tourist towns in North America where the job of a person outside is to offer the customer a gift in return for a ninety-minute presentation of the resort product. I lived in that world for a few decades. It's effective marketing unless you are a woman traveling for a few months who has sold all her worldly belongings and has no forwarding address. This handsome young man told me he was learning English—true—and why doesn't he show me around the area, and then we could have tea—at his shop!

I love sharing this story. It sums up my philosophy on life. *"Life hinges on a couple of seconds you never see coming."* Two lonely souls can connect on levels that defy common sense, disregard age

196

differences, and yet somehow are destined to work. There is no explanation for the instant attraction of a very young man and an older woman.

After two days, I would continue with my journey. But over the next couple of months, I received daily messages: "Come back to Istanbul." It was that final message that sealed it for me. "I know I am poor, but I have a Big Love to give." I was ready for a Big Love even if I didn't recognize it at the time.

It's these moments in life that change our destiny. I'm grateful for this man in my life who took care of me during the pandemic. He made sure if he was busy, his best friend would take me to the doctors so I could get my vaccines or help organize my papers for the government. He did my groceries, kept me from panicking, and was there for me even when he was not there for himself after his father died from Covid-19. When I would question our relationship, he would simply respond, "It is our destiny."

One day I asked him, "why me?" He looked at me, his heart open, eyes wise beyond his years, and responded.

"I could see you were starved for love."

Sometimes you don't know what you are missing until you find it.

28

VULNERABILITY

Brené Brown says it best:

"Owning our story can be hard but not nearly as difficult as spending our lives running from it. Embracing our vulnerabilities is risky but not nearly as dangerous as giving up on love and belonging and joy—the experiences that make us the most vulnerable. Only when we are brave enough to explore the darkness will we discover the infinite power of our light."

Society would frown on my story. Many would speak behind my back. They might not understand the moments I've run away from the sadness that permeated the dark times in my life. I never questioned my decision to leave my husband with two teenage boys when I went to live in Mexico. I believed I was saving my own life, getting out so I could breathe and find self-love again. I'd become a slave to a career that was no longer satisfying and a life that left me emotionally drained. I'd always been the primary breadwinner in the family, and I continued to take care of the financial matters after I left. I had one son going off to college, and my other boy was a year behind him. But I felt I ran away to save my life. I could no longer live in a house with constant arguments. I thought it would be better for everyone.

Is there some shame attached to my decision? Of course. Men do it all the time, but women generally stick it out. I've since accepted that we are all simply human beings trying to exist in a world that demands so much from us on every level. We go to school and learn the arts and sciences, how to add and how to subtract. But no one prepares us for navigating multiple divorces or a worldwide pandemic. Instead, we live with the shame of our so-called 'mistakes,' when this is simply life. We've been given this dream of a perfect life somewhere along the way. Our expectations are unrealistic when we go out into the world. And if you have been brought up in an archaic religious system that does not accept divorce, our souls are hurt because we feel like outcasts and sinners for the rest of our lives. I'm not anti-religion. I'm simply confused by what I was taught and how it fits into the world the way it exists today.

"Wholehearted living is about engaging in our lives from a place of worthiness. It means cultivating the courage, compassion, and connection to wake up in the morning and think, "No matter what gets done and how much is left undone, I am enough." It's going to bed at night and thinking, "Yes, I am imperfect and vulnerable and sometimes afraid, but that doesn't change the truth that I am also brave and worthy of love and belonging." **Brené Brown**

And the most challenging of all of this is self-love

29

ALWAYS BE GROWING

"When I was a kid...."

I was taught by the nuns that self-love was 'selfishness' and selflessness was a virtue. I would say today that both are virtues and have a place in our lives. One cannot exist without the other. I searched the internet for suggestions and ideas that we could incorporate into our lives. These last couple of years have left a deep impression on your psyche if you are anything like me. Some of you have 'fallen apart.' I certainly have my share of insecurity and fear. Others have split with their partners, fought with their families, quit their jobs, or lost them.

I've compiled several great suggestions to help us navigate these times.

1. **Stop comparing yourself to others.** This can be a difficult one to conquer. The advertising world has a knowledge of human nature combined with their use of technology that has us comparing, shopping, and consuming at rates

the world has never seen. This is a dangerous and empty black hole. *Things* will always be a short-term fix. Beware.

2. **Who cares what others think?** This is not a time to worry about petty differences, envy, and jealousy on our planet. Let it all go.

3. **Make mistakes.** It's okay. We all do. Forgive yourself and move on.

4. **Beauty is an inside job.** Recognize that the things that make us beautiful are inside. Religion teaches us it's selfish to be self-centered. But if we don't love ourselves first, how can we be there for anyone else?

5. **Toxicity.** Delete toxic people and thoughts from your life.

6. **I'm okay. You're okay.** We're all afraid. Accept it and do the best you can at the moment.

7. **Trust your decisions**—even when you are wrong.

8. **Don't wait for life to happen.** You are your life. We now know tomorrow is not promised, so live for each day.

9. **I am.** You are the only constant in your life. Be gentle and kind with yourself.

10. **Live. Love. Laugh.** Feel it all. You only live once—as far as we know.

11. **Voice it.** Let your ideas be heard. Living a small life never served anyone.

12. **Stop to smell the roses.** Remember where the best fertilizer comes from. It's necessary to help in the growing process.

13. **Nurture yourself with beauty**: thoughts, experiences, and people.

14. **Forgive yourself.** Be kind. Be patient. You are only human.

15. **Remember to SMILE.** Resting 'bitchface' is ugly. Frown lines lead to Botox, and Botox is expensive!

30

RANDOM MEMORIES
AND THOUGHTS

I was born at 3 am on March 18. My due date was March 17, St. Patrick's Day, the patron saint of Ireland. I started my life one day late and have kept that thought in my mind my entire life. My mother wanted to name me Patricia. But I understand her sisters vetoed it. There were far too many Irish jokes about Pat and Mike (my older brother's name). Instead, I was named after the number one song at the time: Linda.

I was very young, yet I can remember my mother singing this song at parties. I have no idea why I remember a couple of the lines of this song. But I can "hear" my dad playing the piano as I write this. It's one of the cherished memories I have from my childhood.

When I go to sleep
I never count sheep
I count all the charms about Linda
And lately it seems
In all of my dreams
I walk with my arms about Linda

But what good does it do me
for Linda doesn't know that I exist?
Can't help feeling gloomy
Think of all the lovin' I've missed

We pass on the street
My heart skips a beat
I say to myself, "Hello, Linda"

If only she'd smile
I'd stop for a while
And then I would get to know Linda

But miracles still happen
And when my lucky star begins to shine
With one lucky break
I'll make Linda mine

I've tried so hard to find good memories of my early years. I know
my teenage years weren't happy because of my alcoholic father
and conversations that ended as arguments and endless tears.
Occasionally, I get a glimpse of something wonderful from my
past, which will have to do for now. If it really bothered me, I
could go for hypnosis or regression therapy to deal with the sadness
that I carry. Over the years, I've simply buried the thoughts—
whatever they are—and life continues. I've learned my lesson: If
you build a thick enough skin, it's easier to walk away from bad
relationships or an unfulfilling life. I still haven't decided if that's a
good thing or not.

We all have faults and our challenges. I forgave my father a long
time ago.

I don't really have a sense of family connection. That's why it's so important to keep an emotional balance in my life. I don't remember my grandmothers. I can see them in photographs, but it's not the same. I think that has to do with my military upbringing. We spent many years away from Lindsay, the small farming town where my mom and dad were born. And that's where the extended family lived. I wouldn't have seen them as much as we would have liked.

I have two other female cousins born the same year as I was, one from each of my mother's two sisters. I would see them maybe once a year when we would leave western Canada and travel to Ontario to visit. Betty and Susan were born the same year as I. Cousin Susan had a brother named John. He was my first love—I was probably around eleven at the time. I doubt I ever told him that. My adoration was from afar. I know this is a rambling slow-motion visit to my past. Indulge me. I'm testing my memory. Many parts of my mind have taken a hike since Covid began. If that's the worst thing that happens during this pandemic, I will consider myself grateful. On the other hand, as I write this memoir, many parts of my past have come back to visit.

I'm a long way from that small-town farming community in Lindsay, Ontario, where I was born. I'm at my Starbucks "office" (on the patio) listening to the Muslim Call to Prayer this late Tuesday afternoon in Istanbul. And now I've put in my earphones and I'm playing Coldplay's Yellow, repeatedly.

I know my friends can't understand why I write at Starbucks. But it attracts an international crowd and I've made friends here. One is a man, Murat. He's 40 and sells real estate. His stories give me information about how business is done in this country. Many things I'd already discovered in my research. A great deal of residential and commercial real estate is purchased by foreign buyers. It has a lot to do with citizenship. The investment must be paid for in cash, not mortgaged, and have a minimum value of USD 250,000. (Today, April 14, 2022) the Government raised that amount to USD 400,000!) Even though we are in the Middle East, a Turkish passport is valuable. I've learned that a Turkish document will allow you to get a visa for the USA—everyone's dream. Murat's customers speak a combination of Turkish, Arabic, and English. Most are bilingual or multi-lingual. I rarely discuss where the money comes from, but the big projects he deals with, like hotels and office complexes, are cash, not wire transfers *but money-filled suitcases.* I have no idea what conclusions to draw from that piece of information. In this part of the world, many business deals are done in cash. The logistics to handle millions of dollars in cash must be intriguing. I have no idea how this is done. There is so many layers to this country. In the West we deal with banks, wire transfers and this thing called 'mortgages.' Business in Turkey is a whole different ball game.

In another recent conversation, my Real Estate friend explained that he often helped his clients with their shopping. He mentioned that Arab women rarely try anything on. They have no idea if it will fit! If they like it, they buy it. If their weight goes up or down, they always have something that works! That's his conclusion! Furthermore, they don't use credit cards. They carry stacks of cash in their handbags. Every single day I learn something new. Intriguing. Istanbul is an author's dream.

The traffic on the main street in front of me is heavy, non-stop, yet strangely quiet. When did cars become so silent? At this hour, my Pike black coffee has turned cold. It's a chilly spring day but we are on the Bosphorus and the Sea of Marmaris, so the heat lamps on the patio outside are enough to keep the chill off.

Omicron numbers have gone through the roof in Istanbul, but I haven't heard nor seen an ambulance yet this afternoon. Usually, one will go by while I write, which lets me know how intense the numbers will be that night. No one believes the official Covid figures in many countries. I think they might be correct. I won't even hazard a guess why the numbers are being fudged. Omicron cases are slowly moving up again. But 26k new cases in Türkiye are not 100k as in France yesterday, where my young grandson lives with my son and DIL. Five days later, the cases are over 70K in Türkiye and will surpass 100K before they begin to lower again. Masks will be back, but that's something you really don't have to tell the Turks. Everyone conforms. It's never been a subject that caused a debate.

Planning vacations, or visits to Paris to see my son and his family, has been impossible for the last couple of years. This is our life, our new normal. This past week, I received a message that the three tested positive (including my 5-year-old grandson). The good news is the adults are vaccinated, and no one gets very ill. My little guy has some stomach issues and an earache, but he's not sick from Covid.

Don't you feel like this craziness is never going to end? Welcome to 2022. When you think there might be a window of light, another mutation shows up, flights are canceled, and the service and hospital staff are again overwhelmed worldwide. These medical people are genuinely our modern-day saints. It's the physical toll and emotional trauma they must experience, knowing that they will deal with death every day. On top of that, it will turn out that there are cases of physical abuse against the medical staff. Attacks on the very people who are trying to keep us alive will become mainstream.

As a Pisces, I'm strongly intuitive. I pull from various mystical arts, including Numerology. That's why I followed my instincts and flew to Sedona, Arizona, to work with a Shaman when I had an incurable heart condition and was given 6 months to live in 2008. I was destined to meet Akal, who helped me heal my heart. My curiosity about all things mystical makes me automatically see an apparent reference to something like the repetition of the number 2 in the year 2022. My mind immediately goes to the art of Numerology, developed by the Greek mathematician Pythagoras. So, what's in store for us in 2022?

Numerology number 2 is known to numerologists as a supremely feminine force representing both grace and power. It is cooperative, always aiming to bring peace and balance back to a relationship or situation. This numerology number is also susceptible—of all the numbers, it has the strongest intuition. It can sense currents and feelings instinctively, then use these clues to connect with others empathically.

At the core, the 2 in Numerology represents partnerships—the coming together or balancing of two individual people, concepts, or things. While it holds great power over any situation, it wields it with diplomacy and tact. The result is not control and authority but harmony and teamwork. It is a mediator, able to see two sides of a situation unbiasedly and guide others down the middle road.

Intuitive: This number can pick up on energies that cannot be seen, only felt on a deep and subconscious level. This trait allows the number 2 to be instinctually aware of feelings, thoughts, hopes, and fears others haven't expressed, then use them as opportunities to offer support and compassion to the partnership.

Unifying: The *2 in Numerology is a peacemaker* keenly aware of the values of cooperation and working together. It is diplomatic in its dealings because to be anything else would create imbalance. Even when up against contrasting energies, this number sees how the differences can join to create something complete and well-rounded.

Influential: The *2 hold a tremendous amount of power* over situations and relationships (love and otherwise) but handle it so carefully that their influence can go almost undetected. It's like it's working behind the scenes: no one sees it happening, but the results are undeniable. It does not have to push or use force with others because its incredible abilities of compassion and cooperation influence them to follow its guidance.

It's strangely prophetic. If the world is to thrive, we all must learn to exist on this planet as one. Your challenges are mine. And mine is yours. The pandemic has shown us repeatedly that **#WeAreAllOne**.

It's undoubtedly unplanned but perfect that much of my past writing has been on New Year's Eve as the clock turns over into 2022. I wonder what this year has in store for all of us and the world.

For myself, this has been a really challenging year so far. We are into June of 2022, and I am working through psychological challenges and searching for the mental stamina to navigate my personal issues. This manuscript should have been completed months ago. The "2" has turned out to be remarkably prophetic as Türkiye itself is attempting to mediate war between Russia and Ukraine. And just as I predicted, there is no reasoning with Russia.

31

AGGRESSION

I've learned more about myself and life in general over the last couple of years than I have in the previous 70 years. I'm a late bloomer, for sure. I've lived my life backward. Selling everything, buying a series of plane tickets with no return destination—these are things young adults do. But why is an adventure the domain of the young? And here I am, almost three years later, living in the Middle East amid a worldwide pandemic and my own personal emotional crisis. What was I thinking? The answer is complicated, as are all relationships, especially the ones we have with ourselves.

I last attended school a lifetime ago. So, I can forgive myself for not knowing where Türkiye was located on the map. How's that for a pathetic excuse. Even after Chris, my travel planner booked the two-night stay in Istanbul, I didn't open my iPad and check the map for Türkiye. It was only two days, so it would be insignificant in the plan for my journey. Until it wasn't.

I never learned the Turkish language. I allowed my limiting beliefs to be my excuse. It's not Mexico, where tourism is mainly from North America, so most people speak English. Plus, you're taught

French in Canada in school—although I never became fluent. Spanish has similarities to French, and therefore it's easier to understand. Note to self: *cut out the excuses!* But the Turkish language is *complicated!*

I also knew nothing of modern Türkiye. In school, I studied the Ottoman Empire the same way I learned about WW1 and WW11. But that was a long time ago, and my memories are vague. When I arrived for my two-night stay, I honestly thought I was in Europe. I'd met only one Turk in my lifetime. We worked together in Puerto Vallarta. But we never socialized, so I knew nothing about his country. I have enough challenges remembering things if I don't put them in my Iphone notes, never mind recall whatever I had learned about the Ottoman Empire.

Over the last couple of years, I've learned so much about this part of the world. I have a better understanding of the Palestinian/Israeli conflict from conversations with my Turkish and Israeli friends. I now know that Türkiye is in the Middle East, although when I think of the Middle East I imagine camels, sand dunes, men in white robes, and women covered from head to toe in black burqas. And, of course, lots of oil money to spend on a stable full of racehorses and Rolls Royce cars. My wealth of education comes from the movie Sex and the City 2!

But I am my father's daughter, and my curiosity is boundless. Without the internet, I'd be lost entirely. I now understand that Türkiye is different. Outwardly, you wouldn't know the Turks are Muslim. They look and dress like Europeans. The country women cover their heads as my great-grandmother did in the old photographs I've seen from Ireland. The people, especially the young, look like anyone I might see walking the streets of Paris. And in my neighborhood, the young women who are outwardly more conservative cover their hair in a very stylish manner and dress in modest but the latest styles of western clothes. My boyfriend lives in a more traditional part of the city. Some women are covered from head to toe in a black burqa with only their eyes showing. I really don't know enough about the practice to share if the young generation of women from these neighborhoods is covered entirely or not. But most will at least cover their hair. If you doubt that you are in a Muslim country in the Middle East, the Imams will remind you. Their voices can be heard five times a day, reciting the Call to Prayer from over 3000 loudspeakers around the city.

There are many things I've learned since I arrived in Istanbul. Would I have returned here if I'd known of these dangerous uprisings? On July 16, 2016, there was an attempted coup. And as I mentioned earlier, there are still repercussions in the courts from this event. Here's what the **BBC** had to say:

Scores of people have been killed in Türkiye and more than 1,400 wounded in an attempted coup overnight. But who was responsible, what happened and why?

Bridges over the Bosphorus strait in Istanbul were blocked by troops late evening local time on Friday. Fighter jets and helicopters flew over the Turkish capital, Ankara, and gunshots were heard.

Soon after, Prime Minister Binali Yildirim announced that an attempt to overthrow the government was underway.

A faction of the army then said, via a state broadcaster, that it had seized power to protect democracy from President Recep Tayyip Erdogan.

Supporters of Pres. Erdogan took to the streets as the night developed.

A curfew, martial law, and the preparation of a new constitution were announced. Pres. Erdogan, who was on holiday in a seaside resort town, called on his supporters to take to the streets in protest, and he returned to Istanbul.

Throughout a violent night, TV stations were raided by soldiers, explosions heard in Istanbul and Ankara, protesters shot at, the parliament and presidential buildings fired upon, a military helicopter shot down, and the Turkish army chief was taken, hostage.

The army faction needed public support or wider military backing for the plot to succeed. Neither materialized. Opposition parties also condemned the coup.

In the early hours of Saturday morning, groups of soldiers involved began to surrender. Troops abandoned their tanks with their hands up.

Who was responsible for the coup attempt on July 16, 2016?

Before I answer this question, I must add that military service is compulsory for one year when a Turk turns sixteen. So, the urge to fight for what you believe in is not something a Turk would shy away from. But whoever was responsible for the coup attempt on July 16, 2016, is still an ongoing international debate.

The government has blamed **Fethullah Gulen**, an influential, reclusive US-based Muslim cleric) whom it accuses of fomenting unrest. (In 2022, Gulen continues to be under the protection of the US Government.)

Mr. Gulen denied the claims and condemned the coup.

Meanwhile, the Turkish government has arrested some 6,000 people, including high-ranking soldiers and judges.

How has all of this affected today?

In the winter of 2022, news that Russia had begun its Ukrainian offensive was revealed. I'm writing this at my *office* on the patio at Starbucks. I look up to reflect on my surroundings and life in general. I'm surprised at what I see. I reach for my phone to take a photo, then think better of it. An unusual looking military camouflaged Jeep passes on the roadway less than 6 meters in front of me. The turret holds a machine gun. And all sight of the inhabitants is obscured as there seem to be no windows on the side. It's not the first time I've seen military vehicles on the main street, but it makes me acutely aware that Türkiye is both the peacekeeper and the hunted in this part of the world. Every day in the nightly news report, terrorists, or members of groups "designated as terror groups," are raided and arrested in Istanbul or Ankara. According to the Turkish government, Fethullah Gulen is behind these terrorists and any future coups they may plan. Türkiye continues to attempt to extradite Gulen from the US, but the United States will not cooperate.

My life is a prime example of being careful what you focus on. I've been writing about terrorism and various illegal activities in my Code Raven fictional series for several years. The Istanbul Conspiracy and the Istanbul Heist are centered in this fascinating city. I usually base my stories on a factual event. Or something I've heard about or imagined happening in this part of the world. But in my wildest dreams, I never thought I would end up living in a country like Türkiye. I feel like I'm in the middle of one of my novels! But, as James Redfield says: "Where attention goes, energy flows."

The sight of the tank has thrown me off. A lot has gone on in Istanbul this past week. There must be important meetings or foreign dignitaries in town because I see the official black cars moving swiftly through the traffic in front of my "office." I'm sure the cars are all armored and contain security for the persons inside. Although the city of Ankara is the head of government, I am a couple of miles from the Dolmabahce Palace, where many high-level meetings are held. I don't follow such events. But sometimes, when I see a lot of government traffic and police patrols, I go online to see what's up. The news is relatively transparent but might be reported after the fact for security purposes.

I had a 'feeling' something might happen in Istanbul on New Year's Eve. I'm happy to write that my instincts were completely wrong. Istanbul and the rest of Türkiye rang in the New Year in style with outdoor fireworks and parties that lasted long into the early hours of the morning. No terror attacks were reported. But I must have sensed the tensions developing in Ukraine. I began to feel I should get on an airplane and leave the country. But, we were just coming out of Covid restrictions, and each country had different rules for travel.

It wouldn't take long to build up troops along the Ukrainian border. No matter what Russia said, I knew that war was coming. And within a month, it would become evident that the alleged military exercises would erupt into war. When I first read what was happening, there was no doubt that the power of a peacemaker could not stop what I could see coming.

Unfortunately, my predictions have come to pass. As I edit my manuscript today, high-level talks are held between Russia and Ukraine up the street from me at the Dolmabahce Palace! The challenge I see with this meeting is the one in charge of Russia is not present. And as an aside, a hit squad of mercenaries is attempting to assassinate the President of Ukraine. It doesn't sound like the aggressor is negotiating with all his cards on the table.

The President of Türkiye has created a unique role during this crisis. All our hearts are saddened. As I suspected, it will turn out that it was all a stall tactic until Russia had its troops in place. I will never understand what man's obsession is with war. As of the writing of this memoir, the entire world is against the aggression by Russia against Ukraine. I'm currently living in the middle of a Code Raven novel. Where is Luke Raven when we need him?

32

CONFUSED? YOU ARE NOT ALONE.

Here's what Britannica has to say about Türkiye.

*K*emal Ataturk, *(Turkish: "Kemal, Father of Turks") original name* Mustafa Kemal, *also called* Mustafa Kemal Paşa, *(born 1881, Salonika [now Thessaloníki], Greece—died November 10, 1938, Istanbul, Türkiye), soldier, statesman, and reformer who was the founder and first president (1923–38) of the Republic of Türkiye. He modernized the country's legal and educational systems. He encouraged the adoption of a European way of life, with Turkish written in the Latin alphabet and citizens adopting European-style names.*

Türkiye does embrace the European way of life. However, the country has never been entirely accepted by the European Union. The people are proud and hardworking. Many are very well educated, and some are not. It's a country of immense dichotomies, fierce nationalism, and passion. In the last several years, Türkiye has been used by the European Union to stem the flow of migrants to the rest of Europe. There are more than 4 million refugees in Türkiye, easily 5% of the population. Although the EU makes payments to Türkiye to keep the migrants here, the presence of Syrian refugees and other cultures has affected the major cities. Plus, a large proportion of immigrants are here without papers. It's not hard to get lost in a city of 17 million. Unemployment is an issue. But it seems to be an issue everywhere.

From my point of view, I'm not affected by the challenges. When the pandemic began, and the government started vaccinations, I was contacted almost immediately. I'm legal here, but I'm not a citizen. I was surprised at how easily I could get inoculated not once but now twice plus two boosters. I haven't had to use the hospital services. But I imagine they and their staffs are overburdened like all hospitals are in the rest of the world right now. Since I recently had an altercation with some stray dogs. So, I've now had all my shots for rabies? Five trips to a special hospital and very low costs. It turns out I'm fine as the dogs were more than likely tagged and inoculated.

You can imagine that several million refugees are a drain on the social systems no matter how much money the EU gives Türkiye to keep them here. The refugees also take Turkish jobs and work without permits. The wages are low enough without competing with someone who can perform work "under the table." There is social anxiety. It's not felt around me because I'm in an upper-middle-class area. The refugee issue was a challenge from a work point of view, but then along came the pandemic, and with it, some businesses never re-opened, so unemployment must be high. Then in the middle of all this, the lira was devalued, and prices increased. A friend who graduated as a mechanical engineer eleven years ago tells me he is now making less money than when he graduated. The devaluation Is great for tourism. Türkiye was good value before the financial crisis. Now it's incredibly inexpensive to visit a significant first-world historical country. The money issue is confusing and complicated. There's no solution in sight for the average Turkish worker. And yet the people continue to smile.

Ataturk's vision for the Republic of Türkiye was to create a secular society. The population is still over 90% Muslim, so the majority rules. My sweet friend Celine, who passed away last year from Covid, went to the Catholic mass daily. She knew the staff and helped with various church projects. There is tolerance for all religions, as far as I can see. But when you hear about defacing the Catholic Church signage, we must remember that this kind of thing happens worldwide. There will always be a percentage of the population who are anti-anything and anyone different than themselves. We don't have to look further than the Catholic churches and Jewish synagogues that are defaced daily in the USA. Intolerance of religion, race, culture, and gender identity, is a worldwide problem.

There is a culture of kindness in this very macho country. If you follow me on social media, you will see I'm constantly posting pictures of the Cats of Istanbul. When I first arrived in Türkiye, I would walk by the shops in my neighborhood and see the dry cat food and water bowls on the stoops outside the stores. Everywhere I turn, there is food for the cats. I asked my friend about this, and he explained that Mohammad, the Prophet, and founder of Islam, loved animals, particularly cats. There's respect for all creatures. Dogs are tagged, given their shots, neutered, and sheltered in the winter. Cats that one might consider feral really belong to the community. Most are friendly, and sometimes I have the company of one of the cats on my lap while I write!

Do not disturb me! Nap time.

It's late winter now, so cats come into a shop to warm up. Generally, it's not really encouraged. But the one I was feeding near my house finds the inside warmer now that winter is here. She is constantly being led out of the shop and onto the patio. But I noticed the manager had given up. Once she is warm, finds food, and perhaps has a nap, she will leave independently. Last week I had one particularly precocious cat who decided I had been working long enough! You know it's time to take a break when your keyboard is inaccessible!

The stray cats of Istanbul. Obviously, I'm working too much!

I've discovered that the majority of the people in the world are intrinsically good. Most are kind and caring. They simply want to live their lives, find love, care for their families, and have a good time. After thousands of years, you would think we would learn to embrace our differences. As I've said in the past and will say until the day I die, *why can't we all get along?* #WeAreAllOne.

33

GET OFF THE TABLE. MABLE. T
HE MONEY IS FOR THE BEER.

Money is the root of all evil.
Money doesn't grow on trees.
But we know one thing for sure. We can't live without it.

Imagine waking up one morning and watching your earnings and savings become 50% of the value it was the day before. It's surreal, right? How could such a thing happen in today's world? That's precisely what happened in Türkiye towards the end of 2021. I've been mesmerized. It's like driving by a burning building, and you know you must slow down to watch. It's crazy because even though you know that property and even lives are at stake, there is absolutely nothing you can do to help. I'm not an economist, so I don't pretend to understand why the Turkish lira tanked. I'm not sure anyone can explain it adequately. But if I did know why it happened, I would hesitate to put my thoughts down on paper. I only hope it will work itself out.

If you're a Turk working at an ordinary job, imagine your wages are now worth half what they were the month before, yet the prices of most things you need to purchase are based on the value of the US dollar. What do you do? What can you do? Well, if you are rich, you will manage. Life has become very scary if you are an average Turkish family. After all, this is a country that subsidizes the cost of bread for the populace. One might not feel the effects right away, but you can be sure that the grocery stores and all services will go up accordingly in the following weeks. If your wages are worth half and your food costs have doubled, you're screwed.

Rents have soared. This morning, I read rents had gone up 400% in some places. Imagine. And the government just announced an increase in gas and electricity of 10%! I live in a comfortable, rather trendy part of Istanbul. There's tourism, Universities, hotels, and the new waterfront cruise ship project, Galataport. So the effects are not evident in my area. Starbucks didn't raise its prices right away. But after more than a month, the cost of my Grande White Chocolate Mocha is now the equivalent of USD 1.95. A twenty percent increase. Not even close to the devaluation of the lira. And still way below the price of their drinks in either the US or Mexico. I can't see that it has made a difference in their sales. But the average low-earning Turk doesn't come to Starbucks. However, the devaluation has affected the staff. I've doubled the tips I leave. It's a small thing, but I hope it helps. If this issue goes on much longer, I don't know how the Turkish people will manage.

I asked a friend yesterday what a service person like the Baristas at Starbucks would make. He told me about 4500 TL per month. That would be $324.00 US dollars, 81.00 dollars a week. I made more than $80.00 a week at my first job in a retail store in Canada over fifty years ago! With my new rental contract in February, I'm sure that a barista's monthly salary will be less than the new monthly price of my studio rental. But from what I read this morning, the rental increase could be much higher. It turns out my new rent is 6000 Turkish lira from 3700! But with the devaluation of the lira, the rent in USD is still below my original rent in 2020 of 2700 TL. Inflation so far this year is now at 78%! Yes, it's great for someone like me living in Istanbul on US/Canadian funds. But instead, I wish the lira would return to what it was for the sake of the Turkish people I've grown to care about.

I'm not political, nor do I pretend to understand the financial situation. But my heart goes out to a society that was already sick from Covid, suffered the loss of wages with the lockdowns, and is trying to survive on a highly deflated lira. High unemployment is caused by business bankruptcies due to Covid shutdowns, a lack of tourism, and a refugee crisis that allowed illegal employment. But there is one very bright light. If you have no money or lots of money, you can use the mostly free medical system. With a population of seventeen million people, any time of the day or night, hospitals are available for all kinds of emergency. The cost of medicine is controlled by the government. The only drug I can compare it to is the tightly controlled Zanax. The cost in the USA is $238.00 for a box of 30 tablets. The same package of 30 is $4.00 here. I know I've simplified the issue because there are some costs involved in the "free" medical system. But they are nowhere near the developed world like the USA. I do know there is dissatisfaction with the over two million Syrian refuges in this country because everything, housing, medical and food is free for them.

For the sake of the people of Türkiye, I hope this financial emergency works itself out soon. A worldwide pandemic wasn't enough. The blows keep on coming. And yet, the Turks continue to smile.

34

ADVENTURER

*I can choose either to be a victim of the world or an
adventurer in search of treasure. It's all a question
of how I view my life.* - Paulo Coelho

I was okay with aging. Really good. I never thought about it at
all. I went about my life in the same manner I've always done.
If I wanted to travel, I did. If I wanted to get involved with a
younger guy, I did that too. I love to write and share my
adventures with you as well. I published <u>LOVE the Beat Goes On</u>
so you would know that miracles exist because I am one. My story
inspired you, made you laugh and cry, and gave you hope. Then
one day, I left my sales career in Mexico, sold everything I had,
and bought a series of one-way tickets to exotic destinations with
no idea what I would do when I used up the last plane ticket. I
shared that journey with you in <u>CAFÉ CONFIDENTIAL.</u> And
that's how I ended up in Istanbul.

*"Laughter is timeless. Imagination has no age.
And dreams are forever."* - Walt Disney.

I always embraced all those dreams. And I hope I embody the sense of wonder and adventure that I never realized I had until I looked back over my life during the last couple of years. I hope to pass my enthusiasm on to you. If I bought into "I'm getting old," I'd live my life waiting to die. And that doesn't work for me at all! I remember my mother saying: "When I look in the mirror, I see an old lady, and I wonder, who is that old woman?"

I don't see an old woman, not yet. But is this future older lady waiting for me to give up my current lifestyle and accept that I am getting older? Now we've come to the crux of my anxiety. And it may be this realization that threw me into head-spinning panic attacks. I didn't know what was happening to me because I'd never experienced anxiety and panic attacks. It took a visit to a psychologist to understand that the physical feelings resulted from my emotional *dis-ease*.

I thought I had my emotional/psychological crisis under control, but I've been on, and off Xanax longer than I'm prepared to acknowledge. I've learned that my emotional well-being is not dependent on knowing the answers to the "why". If Covid-19 has taught us anything, it's acceptance. We are all human beings doing our best to navigate a crisis we never expected. The fear is there for all of us, no matter how strong we think we are or act. We can do all the right things, or what the medical community is telling us to do, and we can still die.

I couldn't get a handle on what I was doing wrong or what had triggered my current anxiety attacks. If I knew "why," I could fix it. But when I realized if I couldn't find a physical reason, it must be emotional. That's when I began the work I needed to do.

If you've read <u>LOVE The Beat Goes On</u> about my health crisis in 2008, you might remember that after the doctors had tried medication and my heart was not responding, they told me I had six months to live. That's when I took back control of my heart. If they couldn't fix the physical heart, it might be possible my *enlarged heart could have been affected by my emotions.* So, am I back to that place of insecurity again in my life? Did I manage to mask the fear these past years until the ongoing pandemic brought it all back? What if my heart was "swollen"again, only this time the damage might be irreversible? Was I back to reliving the regrets from the past and paying the price for my past actions and inactions? Only this time it reared up as anxiety. It seems so selfish as I sit here writing this. After all, so many have died, so many have come close to death and healed. And many have lost their loved ones, parents, children, best friends, and family

Yes, I had lived through a physical crisis and healed. But maybe this time I won't be so lucky.

And that's when we began talking about various healing arts. We discussed Reiki, and I went for treatments. I still repeat phrases I learned during that period when I'm anxious or distressed. Where medicine leaves off, miracles begin. After several months the Vancouver Cardiologist shook his head and suggested that I ought to get my affairs in order. He said something about *six months to live.* How could that be possible?

I will quickly recap to put it all together for you. By now, some of my close friends at work knew something was going on with me. One of them suggested I go to Sedona. I'd heard of this town in Arizona and the healing vortexes that existed in the mountains. I wasn't a skeptic. But I was scared. I've always thought that there are things outside our comfort zone that we aren't meant to understand. But medical intervention wasn't working. My tests were still the same as when I had been diagnosed months earlier. I was desperate. I booked a flight and advised my superior that I had to go to Arizona. He understood. And I boarded the flight.

I remember heightened anxiety on the airplane. My heart was already swollen, so I was afraid it might burst from the altitude. As we got closer to the region, I looked down at Sedona's unique red rocks, caves, and cliffs. We landed, and all was good so far. When I arrived in the quaint village, a young girl at the reception desk checked me into my room and then asked me if I wanted to do various activities. I looked at her and shook my head. Her friendliness was contagious, so I opened up to her and explained my physical condition.

She looked at me and said, "You need to meet Akal.

My mind has been on strike for most of the last year. I call it my "Covid brain." There are so many things I no longer recall. But I remember her words like yesterday. It's now fourteen years later. I never questioned her. I had no idea who Akal was or what he did. She added, smiling.

"He's a Shaman."

I have always believed in the relationship between the mind and body; I'm a Pisces, spiritual and mystical. Akal had lived in Sedona for many years. Initially, he'd come from Canada. His Raiders of the Lost Ark hat, his walking stick, and a flute were all he had with him. He showed me around the rugged mountains of Sedona, and we ended up at "Airport Vortex." He said a series of prayers and drummed. It was a gloomy day, and I thought it might rain. I don't know what a Shaman does, but I feel that his intonations released things within my mind and heart that opened the pathway to heal my physical heart. The 'how' is not essential to me. The result is what matters. What I do know is after hours spent with this man, I walked down from that vortex, and I felt a lightness in my body and soul. *I knew my heart was healed.*

I know this may sound crazy; but when I returned to Canada, I phoned my Cardiologist and asked him to book me for the heart tests again. He was sympathetic and never asked why. He called me to come to his office when the results were in. He wanted to know what I had done because my heart was no longer enlarged. I told him my story, and he said it was a miracle. I agreed. Maybe the mechanics of my heart were altered by the power and energy of the vortex. Whatever I studied in geography or science in school was forgotten the day after I wrote my exams.

I continued taking medication for my heart and high blood pressure. But my heart was healed. I still drop in on the Facebook Cardiomyopathy support group from Britain to inspire and give hope to those in various stages of this disease. Miracles do happen.

In 2009 I would return to Sedona to say thanks to Akal. It was a stormy day, but we had sunshine in our hearts.

Sedona, Arizona

35

ACCEPTANCE

When I decided to stay in Istanbul for an undetermined amount of time, I went to see a Cardiologist. He did all the tests and was surprised when I told him my story about my enlarged heart. He said I no longer needed any heart meds, just a pill for high blood pressure. He could see permanent damage, but it should not affect me, so that's fine. I've been taking that BP pill for a couple of years. It's kept this sleek, sexy operating machine that might be carrying a few more kilos than necessary running smoothly. You already know how much I enjoy my Starbucks White Chocolate Mocha! If I stopped a few of my bad habits and lost a few kilos, I might no longer need BP medication. But because they call high blood pressure *the silent killer*, I won't play around with that medication without the Cardiologist's approval.

Before I went to the psychologist here in Istanbul, I went back to the Cardiologist and told him about my symptoms. He gave me a Beta Blocker to calm me. I don't like medications, so I cut it back to half a pill to take at night. I would take the SSRI the pharmacist recommended for the day and a half Beta Blocker for the night.

I'm not self-diagnosing (she says as she cuts pills in half and decides when to take them). I would never suggest that. I don't want to overmedicate if it's unnecessary.

When I finally accepted that neither of these medications worked for me, I bit the bullet and went to a psychiatrist. He listened and informed me I had anxiety attacks. He told me to continue what I was taking and added a pill to take for the next 28 days. As I mentioned earlier, it turned out to be a low dose of Xanax. And of course, my fear took over and I flushed it down the toilet! You see, I'm repeating myself. It goes with this challenge I'm having with my lovely headspace. If you come from the US, you know that Xanax is considered a very addictive and dangerous drug. It's controlled here in Türkiye also. I was so afraid to take it. I know that might sound crazy to you, but for a girl who neither drinks nor smokes, never had a joint of marijuana, and won't put anything into her system that she doesn't understand, Xanax is a terrifying word. I also must accept that since my father's alcoholism, I feel that drugs are like alcohol. I don't know what I thought would happen when I took the Xanax—maybe I would go into a trance or have visions.

But when I didn't take the pills as prescribed, the other meds weren't working for me. I went back and he gave me a new prescription. My interpreter never mentioned I threw the first pills away. I felt tired, but somewhat normal. I followed the prescription for a few weeks, then cut the Xanax in half. I was good from the beginning of the treatment. I assumed the drug was meant to 'cure' me, so I stopped right near the end of the dosage. I'm super grateful I no longer need it. I decided I would take the low-dose SSRI prescribed by the psychiatrist until I'm sure my

anxiety is under control. I know I've told you all this before, but bear with me.

That was back in December and January. The mornings were still a challenge. I still dislike my dreams. My nights are like going to a drive-in movie. Gigantic, in your face, drama! These movies are worthy of Academy Awards, or at the very least, we could add them to the Netflix episodes they are based upon! They're vivid and life-like to me. In my dreams, I've been worldwide, from India to the US, the Middle East, and back to Mexico. I get to play characters I might not wish to be in my waking life. I've partied with the Real Housewives of Beverly Hills and gone to Doha, Qatar, with the Bollywood Wives. Last night, I was redesigning interiors in a luxurious mountain home in Colorado. If the dream is troubling, I can usually wake myself. I get up, play a word game on my phone for distraction, and then go back to bed. And if it's anywhere near my wake-up hour, I stay up, shower, meditate, then hit the yoga mat and move into my day as best I can. I've found that morning routines ground me. I tell myself I'm the Boss Bitch of my day, so it's up to me to go through an exercise schedule and eat healthy food for my headspace.

I use my mantra to fall asleep at night and anytime I feel 'off' during my waking hours.

I am life
I am love
I am joy
I am abundance
I am peace
I am healing

This is a mantra I used on my heart when the doctors said it was incurable. I recalled that prayer to stop an anxiety attack that came on suddenly as I crossed the street. Can you imagine how many times I repeated this in 2008 that I can so easily pull it up in my mind today? Last night I said it using the Tapping technique and fell asleep right away. It worked in 2008, and it's working now. The mantra comes to me before I know I need to say it.

Last week I returned to the Cardiologist in Istanbul for an annual checkup. She said everything was normal. I told her I wasn't a fan of the BP med I was taking. I routinely had very low readings. She said to cut it in half. It turns out that one-half of the dosage is keeping my pressure in check. My BP readings are a little low but where they should be to stay healthy.

I'm grateful for the good habits I've developed since my physical heart broke in 2008. And more than anything, I'm thankful for the gift of life.

36

IT'S SIMPLY NOT POSSIBLE…
I'M IN SHOCK

I can't believe I turned 75 in March!

H ow did this happen? How is it possible that the numbers on my birth certificate are entirely nothing like how I feel? I had absolutely no expectations whatsoever. However, each generation has faced its own challenges and has forged its own way. Mine is no different.

If someone had told me 30 years ago that I would be in a relationship with a young guy, I would have fallen over laughing. It wouldn't be because of the young guy. It would be because I could not imagine ever hitting my 70s. However, we expect the rich and famous to get into crazy romantic situations like this, but we can't imagine it happening to ourselves. And it's three years now since my relationship began.

So let me answer some of your questions. The main one is that he has no idea how old I am, nor does he care. It's almost three years since we met, and the conversation about my age has never come up. He's also the most loving partner I have ever had. He's a Pisces like me. We are hopeless romantics. Our text message declarations of love never fail to lift me up if I'm having a challenging day. And I've come to realize that they do the same for him. Love doesn't have to be limited by age; it's an emotional connection. Like a young man once said to me: *everyone needs love.*

We have lots of firsts together. He was only in love once before. He was in his mid-teens, I think. And she broke his heart. He has a rugged, bad-boy exterior, but his eyes show his emotions. He's jealous. I might tease him about the men who try to pick me up or chat with me on the patio when I'm working at my *office*. But that would be an ego move on my part, and he would be jealous and hurt. He knows his countrymen, so he warns me to be careful. I'm sure many women of all ages have been taken in by the words of love from a Turk. Then they've been left crying on the way to the airport to return to the 'real world.'

But the reality is he came into my life when I was lost. I was on the trip of a lifetime, but I had no idea where I would end up after I used all my tickets. I can't explain why I feel that nowhere is home for me or why I keep on moving. Am I running away? If so, from what? I know that despite the pandemic, and my emotional mess this past year, I'm happy in Istanbul. But if you ask me where home is for me, I have no idea what to answer. I usually say, "I'm a Canadian."

I don't think he ever thought I would return to him and Istanbul. But he kept messaging after my two days here, and his final message spoke to my heart. *I know I am poor, but I have a big love to give.* And I knew in my heart that his words were true. His love has surrounded me and shielded me from the loneliness I felt, even if I didn't realize it at the time. He saw things in my "ocean eyes" that I could not have explained.

I wrote before that he comes from the country, although he grew up in Istanbul. His family was poor but very hard workers. His four brothers are very successful. Dad taught them well, and Mom doesn't tolerate any nonsense. But in this Muslim religious family, I'm not acknowledged because it would not be acceptable to have a girlfriend. But you could have a friend that you are engaged to marry. I don't know the customs of the Muslim faith. But I know that if there are rules about girls, alcohol, and cigarettes, my guy has broken all of them!

I'm independent, and I could have gotten through the pandemic without him looking out for me. But there is something special about being *cherished.* Emre made sure I had food and water and stayed in during lockdowns. He visited and cooked for me, but we kept our distance and wore masks. He organized everything so that I was registered for health and got my vaccines when they first became available in Türkiye.

He made me feel safe and loved. *He took care of me.* No one had ever made me feel that way before. And I was there for him when his father died. The family stayed together to mourn the death of the head of the family for thirty days. It's almost two years later, and the pain is still in my boyfriend's eyes.

I guess what I'm trying to say is I found a bad boy who has the biggest heart. He once told me, "My heart is soft." I didn't understand what he meant at the time. I always figured he was with me for the easy sex. But he didn't need me for that. There are always plenty of single female tourists in Sultanahmet. After three years, I can comfortably say he's in it because he genuinely has a 'big love' to give. I didn't know how much I needed it until I found it.

Sometimes I talk about the future. I know one day he will marry and have babies. He will be the most loving father. But his life is far from settled. And the insanity that we have all experienced in the last two years has further disturbed everyone's business lives, including his. Life will have to be much more stable before he can consider looking after a wife and bambinos! So, he has his nieces and nephews to love. And he has me.

I know this is very personal, and you wonder about sex with a younger man. Well, it's like sex with anyone. Except, everyone is different. I've always been sexually active, but it's not the most essential part of life. Friendship, silly conversations, laughs, and being there for each other when life gets messy is what really counts.

I don't know his family, but they know about me. His mom is very religious. Since she lost her husband in 2020, she has spent even more time praying the Quran. My friend lives with his mother, as do traditional Turkish men and women until they marry. The family has not acknowledged me, but one daughter-in-law follows me on IG, apparently. So, she must have told Mom about my existence. Not too long ago, out of the blue, Mom asked her son: *How is your friend doing?* Do you think my Emre might be her favorite? She seems to accept that he might have ignored some rules by having me in his life. But she is a country girl from the village who married at 16. She's not worldly at all. So, she assumes that I am *only* a friend. It's kind of sweet. I have no resentment toward their traditional values. But I do have a lot of sadness that his mother is a widow at such a young age.

Life is so unfair. We've all lost loved ones to Covid-19. Not to be a downer, but all the things the hippies and activists worried about have come to pass. Climate change, disease, famine. We know we must change our ways. But I imagine every generation says the same thing. Anything is possible if we work together to make the change. But first, we must begin from a place of love and accept that we are all one.

We had a bit of drama this week. I hesitate to write about it, but, as usual, I'm an 'open book.' Emre has been relatively aloof, not feeling well, maybe depressed. He had been seeing doctors and going for tests, and the word "cancer" came up. He never told me until he was on an airplane to another major city in Türkiye to see a specialist. When I was trying to figure out what might be wrong with his stomach, I researched. I came across this hospital in Gaziantep, so I recognized the name right away. It's a teaching University hospital, and one of its specialties is Oncology. I've been so fortunate my entire life. Other than a few minor problems I've forgotten about and my "6 months to live in 2008" that I shared in LOVE, The Beat Goes On. I've never had someone I'm close to have cancer.

I was so scared for him. He was quickly and thoroughly tested, and his issue is not cancer. But he, too, is suffering from anxiety. He works in tourism, and when there's a worldwide pandemic, your career trajectory goes down, not up!

We hadn't seen each other in a couple of weeks. Emre didn't want me to know he was ill. He carried that burden inside himself, whereas I would be crying to everyone I know. *He didn't want me to worry.* But he did share with me afterward that while he was in the hospital, he saw a man crying. He went over to console him. The man is under 50, has a wife and family, and has severe cancer. He just found out it's inoperable, and the prognosis is horrible. Hospitals are a reminder how quickly your life can be taken away from you. So, I remind myself with mantras and lists of all the good things in my life. I say them often, especially when I start to feel off.

Unfortunately, my anxiety came back over a month ago. I suppose it was at the time that my guy began to feel ill. I'm dealing with it much better this go around because I know it's anxiety and what I need to do. I know I must eat right and watch my coffee intake. I need to walk, do yoga and meditate every single day. I still play with my meds. I don't want to take Xanax, but the doctor renewed the prescription. Even if it's a super low dose that I cut in half and only take once a day, I really resist taking the drug! I have to watch what I allow myself to read online. I can't solve the world's problems, so I need to stop reading about them. I'm getting much better at this. But I know I will get through this because I can still write!! Without my conversations with you, I would be lost.

Yesterday I went to the therapist. I felt I needed someone to help me understand *why* this feeling was lingering. After all, I'm surrounded by people when I write at my "office," and they all seem to be functioning just fine. When I finally sat down with her, she asked me many questions. I talked and talked about when I began to feel this way. It turns out it all started when the building beside me was deconstructed. I didn't understand what was going on. The men worked until midnight most days, in the dark, and I was afraid. I acknowledged that fear out loud for the first time. I could imagine the workers coming on my small patio, breaking into my flat, stealing my money or bank and credit cards, or taking what they wanted. Of course, nothing ever happened. But that's when my problems began. On top of the Covid fears, that event hit me so hard. It took me a couple of months to identify the problem, but I had never really focused on the "why?" I was feeling so off.

At that point in the therapy, I understood if I needed one word to describe my overall dis-ease it was *fear.* I know I'm coming out of the fear because the men stopped working when they finished gutting the building months ago, and they've since disappeared. But the damage was already done in my mind. I didn't recognize it at first. I now know what I need to work on, and I will find ways to work through this with whatever it takes to find my equilibrium.

Of course, Covid got worse for the world. Even though I tried not to think about it, the fear was still there. And I fought my anxiety. Maybe now I can see it was partially paranoia too. Whatever it is/was, the primary block in my mind was the stigma I attached to mental versus physical dis-ease. After all, when we break a bone, we don't blame ourselves for not being strong enough to avoid the break. Even as I write this, I've gained a new awareness of the prejudice I have long held toward addiction. And I attached the same thinking to mental/emotional illness. Maybe this is a life-lesson I need to learn.

Emre and I both know that we are lucky. The drop in his income because no one was traveling led to his physically stressed body. He's also grateful he didn't have anything that couldn't be fixed.

I always believed that when you are healed from something, the best way to say thanks to whatever or Whomever you believe in is to live your best life. Give back in any way that you can. In some small way, I hope my words will give you inspiration for anything you might be facing in your life right now. You can say with me: "this too shall pass."

I'm editing and trying to make sense of this convoluted memoir that I'm writing for you. I checked the number of pages and saw the word count at 55555! If you haven't noticed, I write in a kind of stream of consciousness. You must know I simply had to look up the numerology explanation of the number 5:

Numerology 5
Number 5 in Numerology **represents the planet Mercury and is associated with our senses**. *These people are usually lovely and have a charismatic aura. They are fun-loving, zealous, and*

cheerful. That is why people love to be around and spend time with them.

I think that's a message to me *to lighten up*! Let's go back to something less depressing for your reading pleasure!

37

IN PRAISE OF OLDER WOMEN

We like to think we are forward-thinking in North America, but other countries in the world ahead of us in many ways. Of the 10 most populous countries, the United States, Russia, China, Mexico, and Nigeria have never elected a woman leader. That's an interesting fact, isn't it? I've never been an activist, at least not outwardly. Instead, I like to think that I've led by example—both good and bad examples. We tend to learn from both.

I would love to live another fifty years to watch how the young women of today will become the leaders of tomorrow. Will women use their power to highlight what wars do to families and possibly pave the way to negotiate peace instead of constant war? Or is femininity a myth? By the way, I wrote this sentence and chapter before Russia invaded Ukraine. Will gender 'roles' disappear entirely in the next generation? We've come a long way. But as a woman, we have a unique point of view and should not be afraid to use our voice in politics.

I read something in the gossip columns today. Kanye West has a "girlfriend of the week." The story was all over the papers. Why? She seems to be an up-and-coming actress, and Kanye is apparently moving on from the love of his life, Kim Kardashian. Kanye took his new girlfriend on this fantastic date (according to the girlfriend). First, they went to his favorite restaurant, where he had pre-ordered all the dishes. Then afterward, they went to his hotel suite, where he had rooms full of clothing for her from his designer of the week. Wow! She was so impressed and called it a "Cinderella" moment.

At first, I glanced at the article and passed it off. Then I reread it. This is their first week together. On one single date, he has taken complete control of her life. He is making her over in his image of what his woman should look like. Think about it. "This is what you will eat. This is what you will wear." They are still going strong a week later and show up in denim on a red carpet. I wonder who made that decision. It's 2022, and still, a man feels that the 'object' of his affections should fit into the mold he has designed for her. Would the reverse ever happen?

The subtle message is, "I like you, but." should be a warning sign. Be careful, or you might lose yourself while trying to please a man. It feels like a throwback to the 1950s. We've taken ten steps forward, and then we take ten back. Within the month, it will turn out that Kanye and his woman have already split. I read somewhere that she says it was never sexual. Really? If that's the case, sign me up for suites full of designer clothes, fancy dinners, and a week in Paris!

Is this a part of our global political problem? Women don't hold enough power to look at the world's issues from multiple angles, including the family unit. Do you think my cynicism is a sign of age? Or could it simply be that I don't care if anyone agrees with me? I say it as I see it. We need more women in the decision-making roles that affect the families and this world.

It's my story, so I can rant occasionally. But I will lighten it up now. While we are talking about women, let me share an article I read today in praise of older women. It's written by Katy Horwood for Metro Magazine online.

Reasons older women are hot.

Katy Horwood leads with the line:
If you're judging people on sex appeal, rather than having the dewy look of youth about them, you can't beat an older woman. Why?

1-They don't give a s*** and are way overspending their time seeking out validation from other people. Self-confidence is sexy.
2-They're confident in the sack.
3-Their libido is on point
4-Imperfections are sexy
5-They won't bore you
6-They're not going to want to be pregnant by the end of the month
7-They can pay their own way
8-They can afford sexy underwear, which they regard as a life essential instead of an occasional luxury
9-They aren't afraid of communication
10-They won't stalk you on Facebook
11-They won't spend the majority of the evening posting selfies up on Instagram or tweeting about your date

12-They're not needy

13-They don't take themselves too seriously

It's not only 'older women.' There are plenty of trail-blazing young women using their voices to make a change. I listened to the Muslim call to prayer last night, and you know I love to do research. I already knew that Muslims pray five times a day. You can find anything you want on YouTube today, so I watched an Imam make the daily prayers, the gestures, the words, and what they meant. One search led to the next, and I came across a couple of fascinating speeches by young, well-educated Muslim women—one on a TED talk and another at an American conference. One spoke of how she went back to Libya and created a movement that would allow women a voice in their faith. From their position, they were able to change the way women are treated within the Muslim faith in Libya. These young women are modernizing the role of women in the Muslim religion.

Why is this pertinent? It's not simply about religion but life in general. I like to read the reactions and reviews I receive from my writing. In my own way, I think I'm trail-blazing the experiences an older woman can have and how she can show up in our society. As both Muslim women said in their YouTube talks, *We need a seat at the table.* My writings are my seat at the table—even if it's a Starbucks table. I hope when I share my life, younger generations will learn that it's never too late to find love, happiness, wellness, emotional fitness, and most important, self-love. It all comes back to how much you want the world around you to change. It must happen first within ourselves, and then we each must decide what exterior action we are prepared to take to make it happen in the world we inhabit.

I write my memoirs because I want to share this tremendous journey called life. I also spend time on Quora, a vast ask/answer site online. I think every type of question is asked and usually answered on Quora. But I had my first nasty attack on Quora. I was answering a question about older women dating younger men. This woman hated my response and called me a *predator*. The attack was so vicious I felt she must have in some way been involved in a triangle that led to her rejection and pain. Still, I couldn't pass it by. I have never actively gone after younger men, ever. So, it really hurt to be accused of screwing up someone's life. While we are on the subject, pretend we are sitting around your table, and I am sharing my hopes and dreams for you and future generations. Men are welcome to listen to this conversation.

If you've reached my age, hopefully, you will have **developed a dangerous level of self-confidence.** No one can tell you who you should be and what (or WHO) you should be doing!

You know who you are. You know what you want. You have a total intolerance of partners who will put you down, tell you what to do, or steal your joy.

You have learned to ignore your imperfections and embrace your strengths—emotional and physical.

You no longer agonize over the extra ten pounds your body wants to carry. Okay, maybe mine is fifteen now, but who's weighing! I've learned to enjoy my sweets without admonishing myself or forcing myself to diet like I would have done twenty years ago.

You know **it's okay to cry over the fate of the world** and accept that all you can do is your part to heal the planet. You put out healing energy through your thoughts and actions and hope all will be better for the next generation.

You have learned the value of friendships and family. You have accepted their love and have learned to ignore their shortcomings. And trust they will forgive yours.

You know that the perfect anything is a myth. Believing in this fantasy can only lead to unhappiness and self-loathing. It could be career, retirement, men/women, or our relationship with our family and children.

And most importantly, **you've learned to forgive yourself.** You have made lots of mistakes. Some you have learned from, others you will continue to make until the day you die. And that's alright. Perfection is overrated.

Be gentle with your heart. Most likely, it's been busted emotionally more than once and will continue to disappoint you. But don't let that affect your physical heart. Learn there's not enough room in that material or emotional core to carry all the hurt and grudges from the past. It will only weigh you down but also leave you bitter. This sadness and anger will prevent self-love and make you invisible to another potential love. So let the negative emotions go, forgive your past, and cherish the good memories.

Finally, when you enter the last part of your life, my wish is that you have found and lived your joy, whatever that may look like for you.

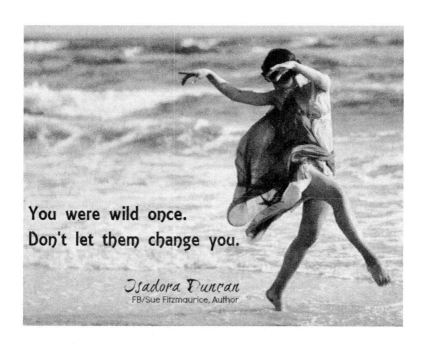

You were wild once.
Don't let them change you.

Isadora Duncan
FB/Sue Fitzmaurice, Author

38

FORGIVENESS

You can't move forward if you are always looking backward.

Forgiveness is a word that most people think applies to what others do to us. But I think it's all about what we do to ourselves. When you think about it, we spend a lot of time talking about the past, especially as we age. Our grandparents called it the "good ole days." I call it history—both good and bad.

It's great to revisit the good things in our lives particularly if we have spent a lifetime living from the heart. But we make choices as we age. We should take the old garbage and incinerate it. If it doesn't serve us now or going forward, why allow it to take up space in our heads and heart. It's like your closet. Imagine if everything you had bought and worn since you were 21 was still in your closet! I'm sure an empty room couldn't hold all of it! Let negativity go if you want to move on with joy in your life. Learn to release the pain, sacrifices, disappointments, and hurt. Then you can make room for the fun that could be in your life when you eliminate the memories that don't serve you. I barely touched on my past marriages or life with my boys' father. What's the point of revisiting the pain, the anger, the things that went wrong? There's no benefit. None. It will always take two to make a marriage work. I'm sure my ex sees things from his own point of view. And that most likely is totally different than the way I see it. But the past belongs in the past.

While we are busy holding on to these hurtful thoughts, they continue to control us. We can't grow nor move forward into loving relationships, including the one we must have with ourselves.

Maybe that's what attracts me to younger men. They haven't lived long enough to be bitter about life. They have dreams and hopes and plans and live in the now. If they moan or complain or carry tons of excess baggage, a person like that would rarely get a second date or be invited into my life as a friend. And that's another choice we get to make as we age. We get to control who we allow into our heads and heart. We can politely claim we are busy when negative people want our attention. Eventually, they will move on. They wouldn't last long anyway. *Misery enjoys company*. I'm not that girl.

The world is filled with goodness and great people. We simply must become the person who attracts those people into our lives. It all starts with a love of self, and only when we love and forgive ourselves can we truly love another. Then we will find our own like-minded tribe.

Be gentle with your failings. Simply because we are older doesn't mean we have found perfection. Just the opposite. Isn't there a Serenity Prayer that highlights this very thing?

GOD
Grant
ME THE
Serenity
TO ACCEPT THE
Things
I CANNOT CHANGE
Courage
TO CHANGE
The Things
I CAN
AND
Wisdom
To Know The
DIFFERENCE

39

SHOULD I GO, OR SHOULD I STAY?

M any years ago, I read that we are all merely spiritual beings having a human existence. I know that's hard to believe because we live on a material plane. And so far, I've never had anyone from the 'spiritual' realm come back to explain what that esoteric world is all about. But let's assume this life is a small portion of our souls' existence. I wonder what this other world would look and feel like. Does this place called paradise exist? Is there really an afterlife?

I was brought up Catholic, so these thoughts were never questioned for most of my life. And even today, I find that the idea of an afterlife is too much for my mind to grasp. I live my life to the best of my ability because this is who I am, who I have become. I've made many mistakes—I call them 'life lessons.' I'm the sum of all those years of religious teachings, life experiences, disappointments, and personal reactions to the things that have occurred during my time on this planet. Having said that, I hope paradise exists. And everyone I ever loved will meet me there.

Do you think we become more cynical as we age? I'm more apt to go with the flow and hope it all turns out. The closest waking experience I've had to the afterlife is my visit from Dr. Wayne Dyer. If you read my first memoir, <u>LOVE The Beat Goes On</u>, you will be remembering this event. Here's what happened. I was sleeping peacefully when I was awakened by the unmistakable voice of Dr. Dyer. I had written my book on my healed heart but was afraid to publish it. I sat on it for a few years. The voice that woke me said: "Are you ready yet?" I never met Dr. Dyer. His voice was so familiar to me from his interviews and online videos. I sat up in bed and laughed out loud. Later that day, I began the process of editing and publishing my first memoir.

I may have had other experiences, but this event was so powerful any others have slipped my mind. As I get closer to the end of my human existence, I know I can't throw away decades of religious indoctrination. To do so would cause irreparable confusion in my psyche. And as you can see from this book, my mind is already challenged! We are the sum of our life experiences and education, both secular and religious. This is all we get to keep us in line, and give us hope that there is a life after this.

I have no fear about an afterlife. I imagine renewed friendships, family, and lots of love. But what if our souls move into another soul about to be born? I don't dwell on these thoughts. I'm simply thinking "out loud" as my mind wanders on this sunny day in Istanbul. What should we cling to, now that we're closer to the end than the beginning? Or should we simply let life take its course and what will be, will be.

Every single day I work on self-love. I evaluate every experience I'm having or about to undertake and question: is it a loving one for me? If it's a morning when I want to skip yoga, I remind myself that if I don't honor my physical body, I will pay for it in the future. Emotionally I believe in second chances, and for some of us, third and fourth. I've learned that there isn't so much love in the world that I can let it pass me by when it is offered. I also know that 'society' cannot dictate what that love will look like. I feel blessed to live during a time when all sorts of love have become mainstream. Same-sex marriage, intermarriage, and blending of existing families are all unions that we can glimpse on reality programs on Netflix and within our circle of friends and families. I hope that as a society one day we will accept all forms of love. It's truly time to broaden our minds and open our hearts. Love is love. *We are all one.*

I've learned a lot from my life in a Muslim country and my experience with international reality shows. I've witnessed the art of matchmaking and whatever other ways various cultures on our planet go about creating marital unions. It all comes down to how we find love and start a family. The old paradigm of my upbringing is no longer the only way humans come together to form a couple. If the statistics are correct, divorce is at an all-time high. It might have a lot to do with our outmoded ideas of hormonal matchmaking without considering all the aspects of what makes a marriage or a relationship work in the modern world.

I'm an educated woman, yet I learn more about how the world's cultures interact and create a family every day. There is no question that love is love, and we are all searching for acceptance and companionship. I only wish I had another fifty years to see how it all turns out. Maybe I could witness a world that truly understands and embraces the concept that people are people. It's not about religion or the color of our skin. We are all made up of genes that sometimes are blended in what we might think are "unorthodox" ways. But what if this is precisely the way we are supposed to be? Only it took us centuries to understand each other. If we are to survive against evil, wars, pandemics, and natural disasters, at some point, we must accept that #WeAreAllOne. We must work together to find the answers to our mutual problems.

However, since I began writing this third memoir, the world is again in the middle of an unexpected disaster.

Only this time, I'm living relatively close to the action. That day I watched the Russian battleships as they returned home through the Bosphorus Strait here in Istanbul, I knew something was going to happen. There were subtle references to troops massing on the Ukrainian border. Yes, Türkiye oversees the Strait. But every instinct in my body said *war*. Of course, Russia denied it. But I've been in Istanbul for three years and never saw Russian warships returning home before. Why would first-world countries start a war with today's ability to annihilate a country with nuclear weapons? Don't we have enough challenges in this world without warmongering? The insanity of the act is so beyond my comprehension. But again, it only emphasizes that the old guard doesn't get it.

Türkiye had no choice. Due to the Montreux Convention signed in 1936, Türkiye controls the Straits. But unless there is a war, Russian warships cannot be stopped from their journey to their registered home base. But once I began to read about the build-up of troops along the Ukraine border, I knew this was not an "exercise." Russia would invade Ukraine. I didn't know that Ukraine had given up its nuclear weapons as part of an independence agreement with Russia in the '90s. With Russia, everything would be a stall tactic until every piece of the military was in place. It's so incredibly sad.

There is zero justification for this military action. The term "third-world-war" is being thrown around. But if it comes to that, the entire planet would be at risk of a nuclear war. This is all so crazy it's incomprehensible. Communications are so transparent today that it's impossible to hide what is happening. No one wants war. But history does repeat itself. And there will always be powerful men (and women) who are so evil that the murder of innocent people is irrelevant. These people have an insatiable appetite for control, power, money, and evil. They have no moral compass. And this is not only a challenge in the East but also in the West. In every generation and decade, these individuals will put humanity at risk.

I was born after the second world war. My father fought for the Canadian Army, but I don't recall him talking about the war. He was in the Signal Corps, so I have no idea if he had to use weapons. I have never been political. I wouldn't participate in a debate on the subject because my knowledge is too scarce. But here I am in Istanbul in the middle of the action while the President of Türkiye is offering to negotiate peace. This is the first time since the late '30s, and early 40's that something of this magnitude has happened in a first-world country. WWII was my parents' generation. The Vietnam war was American. But still, Vietnam was far away and didn't have the same meaning to Canadians as Americans. We heard about it, but it wasn't widely discussed like in the USA. It didn't affect us in the same way. We didn't have access to the information almost instantaneously as we have now. And we didn't have the nuclear arsenal that exists today.

As of this morning's news, Türkiye may become responsible for peacekeeping if a ceasefire occurs. I really don't like the sound of that. It opens the door to aggression or a misinterpretation of peacekeeping action. This will not end well. It feels as if all these meetings are a stall. But for what?

It turns out we didn't have long to wait. Commanders were "relieved" of their command, and new, more brutal men were brought in. The intention became obvious. However, a war of this magnitude with today's ability to communicate means unless Putin is prepared to take on the superpowers of the Western world, he will fail. But then, what do I know about war.

It's been a month since I began this conversation. The information is sketchy, but now the President of Russia is being accused of war crimes. When you think about it, the whole thing is crazy. Millions of people have been displaced. The major cities have been bombed. Even from a purely practical point of view, why bomb cities? The invaders have to re-build them, which will take many years. And a country that's ruined by war, their people slaughtered, families destroyed, will never be loyal to new masters. Due to the location of Ukraine, the relationship between the Russian people with many Ukrainians is familial. The Government asks soldiers to fight their neighbors, possibly even family members. It's insane. Even the Russian Army is against what they've been asked to do. But unfortunately. evil seems to be impossible to control.

At first, I refused to read the news. I knew it would set me back and reverse my emotional health. But my anxiety came back anyway. I know that might be the most selfish thing I've ever written. War close by became one more 'uncertainty' in my life. I won't go into the suffering of a nation, and how I could possibly mention my mental state would be equivalent in any way. But we all see the world through our own lens. To me, there is only one way to stop what is happening. But I will not put my opinion into writing.

I have learned a lot from my Starbucks real estate buddy, Murat. It's always interesting to hear what the country's citizens say about politics. At times like this, I realize I am my father's daughter and sister's sister!! Cathie, my sis, is also an Ottawa political news junkie. My curiosity is in overdrive. But I also know that Türkiye is in a unique position. They straddle the lines between the West and the Middle East. Türkiye is situated in the Middle East and has a major European flair. Russia is 23% in Europe, 77% in Asia. Every day in Istanbul, there are meetings with Dubai, Jerusalem, Russia, or some other European diplomats. Many of those political groups pass by my 'office' at Starbucks on their drive to the Dolmabahce Palace where these high-level talks take place.

We only hear about the conversations that get reported. Bridges have been badly burnt. As of the date I'm editing this narrative, the world feels the pain of the Ukrainians. Many have had to flee, lost family and homes, or died. I genuinely believe that if we want the world and the human race to survive, we must unite with shared values and an end goal of peace. We need to release past grievances and find common ground. Or the world is doomed.

But let's try to forget the war for a moment. Let me share more about Türkiye. The first Covid vaccine was developed by a Turkish couple living in Germany. Türkiye believes that education is essential. There are many discussions about the universities here. In North America, a university education is becoming a luxury. There are scandals about "buying" your way into the Ivy League schools hardly a democratic way to receive an education. The Turkish Government subsidizes or pays for universities. The downside is a doctor or other professionals, must work in a Government-run hospital for the wages set by the Government. The citizens have a considerable advantage as medical is free for the most part. They have no idea what that means in the rest of the world. But for the hospital employees, the wages are meager. It's a complicated situation. But the government education subsidy also means as the younger population becomes better educated, there is the threat of a brain drain. And this year, even more professionals talk about leaving the country due to rampant inflation. The doctors did some type of slowdown or strike here recently. I read that their wages are the equivalent of about $500 a week! According to my Starbucks friends, the minimum wage is around $80.00 a week. I spend almost that much between Starbucks and groceries each week just for myself.

And on top of that, the currency's value is less than half of what it was when I came here three years ago. And it continues to drop. The challenges of all this, plus the added seriousness of the war, meant my friends in North America encouraged me to leave the country. But I think Türkiye is in a unique situation, so why not see how it all plays out? That's the mystery writer side of me talking. It's too bad my fictional Code Raven group can't fix this one.

Elections are coming up next year. The date has not been announced. It will be very interesting to say the least. If you're curious, do the research, and you will understand why. I'm not going to voice an opinion here. People love and hate their politicians all over the world.

40

YOU ARE NEVER TOO OLD.

Let's change the subject from war and wages to something that concerns all of us worldwide. Every day more information is emerging about the health and habits of our aging population. It's both inspiring and daunting.

> "People often ask me if I'm "passing the torch."
> I explain that I'm keeping my torch, thank you very much—
> and I'm using it to light the torches of others. Because only if each of us has a torch will there be enough light."
>
> ~Gloria Steinem,
> Hedgebrook Alumna

D. Z. G. Dinkmeyer posted this on a FaceBook site called We Love Memoirs:

An extensive study in the U.S.A. found that the most productive age in human life is between 60-70 years of age.

The 2nd most productive stage of the human being is from 70 to 80 years of age.

The 3rd. most productive phase is from 50 to 60 years of age.

The average age of NOBEL PRIZE winners is 62 years old.

The average age of the presidents of prominent companies globally is 63 years.

The average age of the pastors of the 100 largest churches in the U.S.A. is 71. The average age of the Popes is 76 years.

This suggests that the best years of your life are between 60 and 80 years. A study published in the NEW ENGLAND JOURNAL OF MEDICINE found that at age 60, you reach the TOP of your potential, and this continues into your 80s.

Therefore, if you are between 60-70 or 70-80, you are in the BEST and 2nd Best level of your life.

SOURCE: N. England J. of Med. 70,389 (2018).

I'm rather fascinated by this study. These past few years have been very creative and productive. I now have 19, and with this, 20 books on Amazon. I liquidated a comfortable life in Mexico and took off on a solo trip I could never have imagined in the past. I visited multiple destinations around the world with no return ticket. I've learned more about the world I inhabit in the last three years than in the previous seventy!

I would not have done these things when I was younger. It would have been a combination of fear of what could happen and a lack of adventure and curiosity about the world. I was too busy bringing up family, advancing my career and working through my personal and emotional problems. But the moment I decided to sell my condo in Mexico in 2019, I discovered what it means to be truly free—or 'homeless' depending on how you look at it!

However, this freedom in the middle of a worldwide pandemic and a nearby war comes with complications. Unfortunately, my emotional balance is shaky.

wildwomansisterhoodofficial   •••

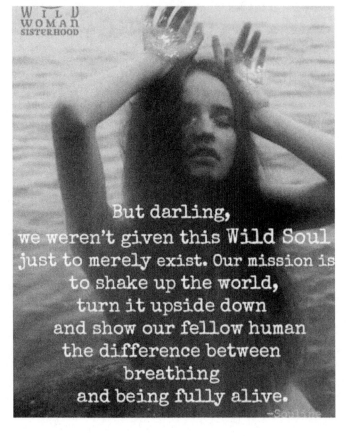

41

UNPLUGGED IS AN ILLUSION.

I'm at my "office" on the patio at Starbucks. It's a rainy Sunday in June and I'm writing. I must chat with my Turkish friends who speak English. And I recently met two young men, one who is Turkish and studied in China and his Chinese friend who is investing in real estate here so he can get Turkish citizenship. You know there's a story I will have to discover from these two guys. And of course, while I'm listening to my friends' chat, I must feed my favorite cat.

Murat, my real estate friend, said he thinks I am brave. I never saw myself that way. But I suppose all my solo travels, the decision to live in Istanbul, a city that is Turkish and predominately Muslim, seemed to be a big thing to him. But these past couple of years of uncertainty and insecurity led to panic attacks and my use of Xanax. So, I'm not sure that I'm brave after all. I suppose everyone's interpretation of the word is different according to their worldview and the people they know.

As I mentioned before, my writing desk is a few meters away from a busy main street that leads to a famous Turkish palace. Even though Istanbul is not the seat of the national government, I can always tell when the country's leader is in town by the not-so-discreet protection vehicles that keep him safe. I've also learned things about the drama that transpired over the past ten years in Türkiye. It's fascinating to hear my friend, an educated professional, voice his thoughts and fill in the gaps in my knowledge of Türkiye's politics. He shares what is reported and what is not. But there is no question that the country is led by a potent individual. He seems to be the only world leader that was able to get Russia and Ukraine to sit down for discussions about a cease-fire. Even if it was all a stall, it allowed thousands of civilians to safely get out of their country. And the rest, well, it's too sad to talk about.

But Türkiye has its own challenges. The Ukraine conflict has been a distraction but not a deterrent. Can you imagine waking up one morning and watching your $1.00 (Lira) become .50 cents? Some economists predict inflation will hit 50% in the first quarter of 2022. And they were right. Mid-February, it's at 48%! And in May, I read it hit 73%! If your income is not Türkiye-based and your money is in U.S. dollars, it's not a problem. You've gained 50% more buying power. You might not notice it right away. After all, you can't possibly imagine that this crisis will continue. Until it does. So that means the cost of gas, electricity, oil, food, and all the necessities of life must increase. It's been a complete roller coaster ride for months now.

I read yesterday that one apartment building was requesting a 400% increase! My increase was more than double. But with the devaluation, I'm basically paying the same I signed on for three years ago. I've been very fortunate. Imagine if you are Turkish, your money is worth so much less, and if you must look for another place to live, the costs will be prohibitive. There are laws, but they are also tied to inflation. Don't even try to understand it. No one thought it would continue, but it's been a few months now. Let's just say the financial drama doesn't look like it will change anytime soon.

Every day is a learning experience for me. One morning I awoke to no internet in my building. The links were there, but they were not connecting to my devices. I panicked. So, I did yoga without Adriene, had breakfast, and headed to my "office." At that point, I was still checking the news every day. After all, how often do you find yourself watching Russian warships on the Bosphorus Strait? At the same time, the U.S. was telling its embassy occupants in Ukraine to evacuate because Russia has the country surrounded! How can I keep up my high level of anxiety if I don't check the latest pandemic predictions or what Russia is doing today? In any case, I ate lunch and slept for a couple of hours.

Then I seriously didn't know what to do. I can't play my games because they are aligned with the internet. I can't read. My books are on my iPad and must be downloaded. No internet. So, I plugged in my computer and turned on my music. And I *danced!* And sang along with my favorite Coldplay tunes. I also compiled my playlist for this book. It will be at the end of Destiny's Daughter if you want to check it out.

Now it's getting close to midnight. I've been snacking, writing and dancing. I'm having a glorious time. This is as "unplugged" as I can get in this tumultuous new world. I should unplug more often!

My curiosity about everything seems to increase with my age. I'm thrilled that my creative outlet allows me to continue to learn and grow. It's also great to mix up your routine. I usually do a lot of

Googling when I write. My memory is not that great—but it never was! I copy and paste and save it on my computer. As my mother used to say, *if you can't remember, it wasn't that important!* Thanks, Mom!

Every single day I learn something new. However, I also have a limiting belief that learning a language is hard for me. Turkish is a real challenge. Now I know how easy it would have been to become fluent in Spanish. But Netflix is a great way to learn. I watch the shows in one language and check the subtitles. I should be fluent in French, Spanish and Turkish, but I'm lazy. I've got some easy Turkish phrases. I was studying last night while I did my pedicure. Lately, I've begun to use Turkish subtitles where available. I should listen in Turkish with English subtitles. That's not going to happen! Eventually, some of it should sink in. I use sign language and pantomime when I need help! Meantime I'm still waiting for all you techies to come up with that language chip to put in my brain so I can understand multiple languages and respond as well!

So that sums up my life in Türkiye. Every day is filled with a new drama, perfect for a conspiracy author. And I have a great plot brewing for my Raven Group. But it will have to wait. While my emotional health is a bit off, I can't get involved with any Raven antics. They tend to get into serious and disturbing trouble.

42

SHADOW LOVE TO THE RESCUE

I've been researching love.

If I look back through my life, I have been in and out of many partnerships; I can't remember all of them. Some were important, serious, and led to marriage. Others were for a season and ran their course. Most couples meet, grow into marriage, have a family, have grandchildren, and live together until one or the other dies. Unfortunately, I've not been blessed to be in that union. It simply wasn't my destiny.

What separates the couples who seem to be able to keep their love and family intact during this century versus the others like me who wander looking for an ideal mate who never seems to appear? Is forever love *'til death do us part* a myth? If I believe in destiny, I was meant to leave Canada, live in Mexico for many years, meet exciting men, fall in love, and be disappointed by love. And finally, for some bizarre reason, end up living in Istanbul, in the Middle East, for the past three years. I've never questioned my destiny before. But now, as I find myself fragile emotionally, I'm asking myself these questions.

When I left my husband and two teenage sons in Canada, I remember I felt I did so to save my own life. I couldn't handle the bickering, the toxic home environment. I could not imagine spending the rest of my life in this situation. I continued my financial responsibilities until the house was sold. But I never once questioned why I left or if I was doing the right thing. Now that I look back at my life, I know I felt guilt, but I also felt if I was to save my sanity, I had to get out.

In my research, I came across the concept of "Shadow Love." There are two sides to love. When two people come together, there are bound to be differences. We grow in our relationships, but it is unlikely that we both grow at the same rate. If we have married young, we might not yet know what we truly want in life. We may grow apart as we pursue our dreams. We may even come to a point where we need different experiences. Those differences can help us grow together or tear us apart.

Growth, emotional and mental, are typical characteristics of the human existence. In our twenties, a person we marry will likely mature in ways we didn't see coming by our forties. It can be harmful or good, but it is a fact of life. It's a foreign thought that we might separate for a period, to explore other interests—and that doesn't mean the subjects are sexual—and then come back together enriched. We can then share these experiences, and both grow from them. But we live in a society that doesn't think a marriage can work this way. 'Growing apart' doesn't have to mean divorce—which is at an all-time high. Being apart may mean: "There are things I want to experience, a journey I want to take, and something I want to explore. But it doesn't mean I no longer love you or want a divorce." We don't stop growing just because we get married. Do you suppose our definition of the way marriage should work could be improved?

Lynda's random thought for the day: life is not meant to be black or white. Instead, relationships, like life, go through various shades of gray.

43

BRAVEHEART

If I had a daughter, what would she think of her mother? Would she see me as an independent woman who followed her heart and dreams? Or would she see me as a woman who kept running, searching for an ideal life that doesn't exist? Would she share my values or curse me for leaving her to deal with her life while I moved to Mexico or traveled worldwide? Or would I have missed Mexico and the world because I had a daughter I could talk with and share my insecurities? Would she have married, rebelled against my nomadic lifestyle, settled in one town, and had three kids? Would she blame me for everything that went wrong in her life? Or might she be my best friend, someone I could turn to as I age and know that she would always be there for me, whatever happened to me?

This past year has been a challenge. I've always been open about my life, but it's easier to talk about my sex life than my innermost heart thoughts. I've discovered what it's like to suffer from anxiety and have panic attacks. I've used medication to deal with my challenges—medically supervised. And during this time, I questioned some of the decisions I've made in my life. I've concluded that the hurts I 'buried' should have been brought out in the open and dealt with at the time. It took a worldwide pandemic to realize that I'm only human. I'm not a superwoman. But the people in my life are not superhuman either. It might have been unfair when I judged them so quickly. I never took the time to understand that we are all in the same universe, doing our best with who we are and the hand we are dealt.

The first time my Starbucks buddy, Murat, said I was brave. I simply shrugged. But lately, I stopped to think about his words. When my heart gave up on me, and the doctor's diagnosis was six months to live, I traveled to Sedona, Arizona, to work with a Shaman. Akal gave me the name: *Strongheart.* I wish Akal was here with me right now. Not only to thank him but to help me find within my heart the bravery required to make my way through this minefield that keeps exploding in my psyche. Maybe it's time for *me* to re-read <u>LOVE The Beat Goes On</u>. I need to remind myself that there is so much more to life than what we can see and touch.

If I learned one thing from my physical heart, I knew I couldn't fix myself without help. I'm proud that I recognized when I hit an emotional wall here in Istanbul. I didn't understand what was going on with me at the time. But I'm grateful I asked for help. I'd managed to survive on this planet for 74 years without anxiety attacks. Welcome to your 75th year, Lynda!

When the medication from the pharmacist wasn't enough, I did my research and found a psychiatrist who explained what was wrong. He put me on Xanax. I still insisted that I control my medication because I am deathly afraid of addiction. I eased off the low dose of Xanax as I felt better, and all was good. I read a lot about what was happening in my body, and I realized that it's not always good to be a superwoman. Sometimes it's okay to fall apart and be afraid. It's part of the human condition. And then I fell apart again. And again.

It came on so suddenly. I wasn't prepared. But at least this time, when that sick feeling hit the pit of my stomach, I knew what it meant. I went back to the psychiatrist. I went with a friend who could translate, and the doctor explained to me that I didn't need to be afraid of addiction. It's interesting that from all my comments, he understood that dependency was my greatest fear. I've been so lucky my whole life. I rarely drink and never smoked, but I do love my sweets. And other than my 6-months-to-live heart diagnosis in 2008, I've been super healthy. Even the lowest dose of Xanax is too strong for me, so I cut the pills in half this time right from the start. After two weeks at a half dose, I stopped taking it. Only when I get that "feeling" do I take a half. It seemed to work perfectly for a couple of weeks. And now I'm back to square one. I know this is not the end of that drama. I have to deal with what is causing my distress. So I have taken the advice of a woman I am friends with from the park and have an appointment with a therapist who speaks English. If I can understand the why and how to deal with this, I know I will get better.

I finally visited the therapist, made a second appointment, and canceled it the next day. I shouldn't be surprised at myself. But I think I need time to work on what I learned. I discovered that I am *consumed with fear*—my words, not hers. I now know exactly when it all began. The demolition of the office complex beside my apartment set me off. I never dealt with the harm it did to my psyche. I'm sitting with this, facing it, analyzing it, and meditating on releasing the fear. And then, I will do video sessions with the therapist if she is okay with that. I almost feel guilty sharing this with you when many of you have gone through so much more. I know you have lost loved ones and have suffered during these last couple of years. I feel a bit lost in my own way, so I hope the therapy will help. But if history has taught us anything, all we can do is pray that this too shall pass.

I did my first video call at 9 am. The therapist asked me questions and took notes. At the end of the session, I said to her, "So, what do you think?" And she responded that she would not come to any conclusions. She would listen and ask questions and take notes. If this is how therapy works, I'm not sure it will work for me. By mid-afternoon, I'd taken the 2nd half of my low dose of Xanax.

This morning I went on a "Therapy research expedition." What is therapy, and how does it work? First, therapy does not fix you because you are not broken. The doctors look at how they will cure you with a medical issue. But emotional therapy, mental illness, or how our bodies adapt to emotional problems is not a disease. Well, it sure feels like a dis-ease to me! But what do I know? I'm not a doctor. I'm simply broken—wait, I'm NOT broken. Maybe my emotional heart is slightly worn out!

Now I understand the role of the therapist. I had breakthroughs when I expressed my thoughts out loud. So, I think I can work within the framework. But I also must accept that this process will take time. And I need to take my medication as directed. Therapy is supposed to help me uncover strengths and learn new ways to deal with my feelings. This whole issue is new in my life rather than a lifelong issue—or is it? Maybe I can work through it and get off the medication with the right mindset.

I will never take "normal" for granted again.

In the meantime, I'm finally accepting I can't get through this on my own. So, it's okay to fall apart for you 'strong' men and women out there. That's why psychiatrists and therapists exist!

But after a couple of sessions, I think therapy is not cutting it for me. I know I say out loud the non-stop chatter that exists in my mind. She offers the odd "How does that make you feel?" As usual, I'm oversharing. But if any of you have gone through or are going through it now, I want you to know that you are not alone. I've also heard it can take time to find the right therapist, and one or two sessions will not cut it. I'm also in a foreign country. So even though the therapist speaks English, is she familiar with my Canadian cultural background? Will she ask the right questions?

The big question remains, how did I get to this age and stage in life without falling apart before? This week I will bare my soul and share my heart with a different psychiatrist. But I feel like I'm wasting time. All they seem to do is listen, ask a few generic questions, then write me a prescription. If I look back on my life, there were many times when it would have been easy to throw a pity party for myself. But I never felt I had the luxury of going down that route. Most of my life, I've made both good and bad decisions. I admit they led to my challenges. But I never had the luxury or would take the time to break down. Too many people depended on me to keep it together. But maybe I did lose it in 2008 but I was busy with work, making trips to Vancouver, and finally working with the Shaman, to realize I'd lost it! I had no time to feel sorry for myself. But I was one of the lucky ones. Destiny and my Higher Power intervened and cured my heart. I will never forget how fortunate I have been.

Have you ever heard the expression: *Be careful what you wish for?* This morning I was re-reading LOVE because Amazon had made some changes to their distribution flow and required that I update my first memoir! As I glanced through each page I was reminded again of that time in Sedona. Akal named me Strongheart. Now I think I will focus on the bravery I need to face the next few weeks or months of my emotional healing. I need so much positive reinforcement when I awake at 5 in the morning and I'm desperate to delete the memory of my nightly disturbing dreams. If only I could control my sleeping hours. This is s a battle I need to wage. And that's going to take every ounce of bravery I can find.

Braveheart will be my new name.

I know one thing for sure. I will never give up. And I know as you are reading these pages you are behind me as I am behind you. Whatever challenges we are facing in our lives. I thank you in advance for your love

44

SO, SERIOUSLY, IF I HAD A DAUGHTER WHAT WOULD SHE SAY TO ME?

Maybe she would tell me to do what the doctor says and stop screwing around! If she inherited my spirit, she'd likely say "you think you know everything, but you don't!" She'd tell me to take the damn medication precisely the way it's prescribed. And she'd tell me to stop googling anxiety and get on with my life. But then she'd remind me that I don't have to be the strong one all the time. Vulnerability is not a four-letter-word. This too, will pass.

If I had a daughter, I hope she would accept Yunus, my Big Love. And she'd love me enough to stay silent when I say age has no meaning when it comes to matters of the heart. Sure, she would think to herself why would I allow myself at this stage in my life to be in a relationship that has no future. Out loud, she might agree that there are no guarantees in life anyways. But most of all, she would accept my life choices because she loves me.

I hope she would sing along with me to *Yellow* from **Coldplay**. I'm playing this music repeatedly because it reminds me of the light

Yunus Emre has brought into my life over the past three years.
But it would also be a song we sing about ourselves.

Look at the stars
Look how they shine for you
And everything you do
Yeah, they were all yellow

I came along
I wrote a song (book) for you
And all the things you do
And it was called Yellow

I swam across
I jumped across for you
Oh, what a thing to do
'Cause you were all yellow

I drew a line
I drew a line for you
Oh, what a thing to do
And it was all yellow

Look at the stars
Look how they shine for you
And all the things that you do

Your skin, oh yeah, your skin and bones
turn into something beautiful
and you know, you know I love you so
You know I love you so

281

I also believe that there isn't enough love in this world to say no when it is offered to you.

And finally, if I had a daughter I hope she would say, "Mom, if you are ever scared or want to settle down, you know you will always have a home with me."

And that, my friends, may be the crux of my anxiety.

I'm sitting on my patio in Istanbul looking out to the sparkling turquoise sea. I will apologize in advance for the numerous references to my emotional disfunction. I keep reminding myself that I am not a superwoman. It's a humbling revelation. The situation has both inspired me and created a personal story that comes from the depths of my heart to yours. We live in challenging times. No matter what you are going through I want you to know you are not alone.

Dalip, you told me to get busy and finish this memoir because my words are like "oxygen" for you. I realize they are also the oxygen I need at this moment in time for me too.

And finally, for all of you, may your beautiful heartbeat continue to live on as mine has for me. We are all destiny's children.

45

MUSINGS

The days are getting longer, and the setting sun is reflected gold on the windows of the three-hundred-year-old Mimar Sinan Fine Arts University across the street. It's time to close my "office" for the night. Streetlights are coming on, and I must make my way home. My sweet feline companion senses my writing time is ending. She's beginning to stir. Yet she is comfy all curled up on my knapsack. I don't have the heart to disturb her.

I feel at peace.

Thank you, again, Dalip Shandil, for reminding me to get busy on my next memoir. You must have sensed my need for the personal therapy and comfort I find when I compose these words. And in the work, I find my balance. Every day I remind myself that I am only human. I've re-read and re-written this manuscript to make more sense for you so please forgive my repetitions. The words come from my heart.

It doesn't matter how many times I fall I know I will pick myself up and keep on going. So let me leave all of you—including myself—with these thoughts.

Life is far too short.

Embrace each joyous moment.

Love your crazy.

Accept yourself unconditionally.

Forgive your children. "They know not what they do (say) Luke 23:24."

Listen to your heart.

Live without regrets.

Trust your magic.

Follow your dreams.

Wherever you end up is where you need to be.

And finally:

Never say no to "big love," or you may regret it for the rest of your life.

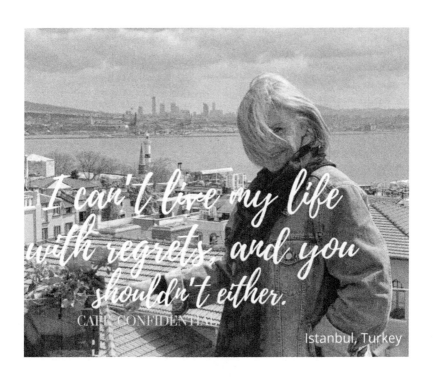

I can't live my life with regrets, and you shouldn't either.

CAFE CONFIDENTIAL

Istanbul, Turkey

GRATITUDE AND RESOURCES:

Yoga by Adriene
Deepak Chopra meditations
Nick Ortner's Tapping Technique to Calm Anxiety & Stress in 3
Minutes
5 Tips to Improve Your Mental Health
5 Lessons to Live By, Dr. Wayne Dyer
Oprah What is your dream for you…
The Most Eye-opening 20 Minutes Oprah
Favorite Deepak Meditation
Anxiety Sadhguru

Private Group JOIN US! We'd love to have you. Lynda's Raven
Army https://www.facebook.com/groups/861045737567359

Watch this every day Denzel Washington

Benzo Addiction tapering off

Books that have influenced me.

I Can See Clearly Now, Dr. Wayne Dyer
You Can Heal Your Life, Louise Hay
Eat Pray Love, Elizabeth Gilbert

Check out this site on FB We Love Memoirs

Lynda's Books:

https://www.amazon.com/author/lynda.filler
LOVE The Beat Goes On 1ˢᵗ Memoir
Café Confidential 2ⁿᵈ Memoir
Code Raven Series
Contemporary Novels
Poetry Books: The Love Fix, Love Rehab, I (Spy) Love

Music Playlist

Ocean Eyes	Billie Eilish
One Kiss	Calvin Harris, Dua Lipa
Bellyache	Billie Eilish
Scars to your Beautiful	Alessia Cara
Take Care (feat. Rihanna)	Drake
Dancing With a Stranger	Sam Smith and Normani
Yellow	Coldplay
Paradise	Coldplay
Fix You	Coldplay
The Sun is Shining	Christien Rosen
Delicate	Taylor Swift
Shadow of Love	Celine Dion
Never in Your Wildest Dreams	Tina Turner, Barry White
Sun is Shining	Christien Rosen
Sideways	Citizen Cope
Get Lucky feat. Pharrell Williams	Daft Punk

Printed in Great Britain
by Amazon

23907171R00165